Last Lunch

Joe
Congratulations on your new job. Hope you enjoy my book.

8/21/2019

WILLIAM (BILL) FUNNEMARK

outskirts press

Last Lunch
All Rights Reserved.
Copyright © 2019 William (Bill) Funnemark
v2.0

The opinions expressed in this manuscript are solely the opinions of the author and do not represent the opinions or thoughts of the publisher. The author has represented and warranted full ownership and/or legal right to publish all the materials in this book.

This book may not be reproduced, transmitted, or stored in whole or in part by any means, including graphic, electronic, or mechanical without the express written consent of the publisher except in the case of brief quotations embodied in critical articles and reviews.

Outskirts Press, Inc.
http://www.outskirtspress.com

ISBN: 978-1-9772-1440-9

Cover Photo © 2019 Bill Funnemark. All rights reserved - used with permission.

Outskirts Press and the "OP" logo are trademarks belonging to Outskirts Press, Inc.

PRINTED IN THE UNITED STATES OF AMERICA

I never planned to write a book. I never planned to be a widower. I never planned on a lot of things. God has a way of making a plan for me. God put Carol and me together and blessed us with a wonderful marriage. This union produced three amazing children. Each of our children found their own special soulmate just like Carol and I did. These marriages have produced nine amazing grandchildren. I would like to dedicate "Last Lunch" to my family. Some of you are mentioned in my book, while a few were not. I don't want to slight anyone. So this is my family.

Carol Jean Leek Funnemark

Stephanie Lynne Funnemark Hamell and Pete Hamell
Connor Patrick Hamell
Daniel William Hamell
Andrew Joseph Hamell

Mickolyn Elizabeth Funnemark Clapper and Trent Clapper
Courtney Elizabeth Clapper
William August Clapper
Trice Funnemark Clapper

Chad William Funnemark and Laura Funnemark
Lainey Elizabeth Funnemark
Sophia Renee Funnemark
Adalyn Lovey Funnemark

Love you
Dad/Grandpa/Husband

Table of Contents

Last Lunch	1
In Conclusion	229
Epilogue	235

Last Lunch

"**My head is** spinning. I think I'm going to be sick. I think I need to go to the hospital, but I'm so dizzy I don't think I can walk." The last words my wife spoke to me before she slipped into a coma, never to wake up.

Carol and I were seniors in high school when we first dated, but we'd been friends for as long as I can remember. We went to elementary school together, went to the same church, and were from the same little town, Wesley, in north central Iowa. I had dated other girls, but at the time of Corwith-Wesley High School's homecoming dance in December 1966, I was unattached. Carol had dated other boys too, but currently was also unattached. It was a mere accident that we even made it to the dance together. I originally had asked Judy to go to homecoming with me, but she turned me down. This was a crushing blow to my ego, but I survived to live another day. Unfortunately, I was still without a date. I decided to ask Carol to go with me, figuring she might go with me just as a friend. Little did I know she'd had her eye on me for some time. Thus, began a romance that lasted for nearly 50 years. A footnote on Judy, many years later, Carol had the gall to accuse me of trying to date Judy just because she had big boobs. I will neither confirm nor deny this accusation.

Carol worked at Algona Good Samaritan Care Center for thirty years, twenty-five as Director of Nursing Services. She retired on January 17, 2014, a Friday, and the following Monday she started working as a nurse consultant. I was still teaching high school science at the same school we'd attended many years before. Retirement for Carol was good. She set her own schedule and was able to travel when she wanted. Carol and I had developed unique travel arrangements over the previous few years and being retired made it even better. Every summer I scheduled a motorcycle trip and Carol would fly to the destination to meet me there. We'd have our vacation, she'd fly home and go back to work, and I would ride home…more or less.

I retired from teaching June 1, 2015. A week later we drove to Myrtle Beach, SC and met our friends Ed and Becky for a retirement vacation. None of us had ever been there, but Carol and I fell in love with the place. In March 2016, Carol and I revisited Myrtle Beach. I signed up to run the Myrtle Beach Marathon on the 5th, and since we were both retired, we could take off as much time as we wanted. We really enjoyed the town and the resort, Ocean 22, that we stayed in. After a week in Myrtle Beach we drove to Orlando to spend a week with Stephanie and her family and then jaunted back to Iowa. Carol went back to her consulting work and I started a long-term subbing job at Baxter High School, teaching most of the science classes for the rest of the school year.

Carol and I spent a few more vacations together, but in October 2016 we planned another visit to Ocean 22 with Ed and Becky. Carol and I planned to drive to Texas to celebrate Connor's birthday and then proceed to Myrtle Beach, spend a little over a week there and drive home. Even though Carol was retired and her consulting job was part-time, she just didn't feel she could be gone that long. Her clients needed her. She informed me, "If I fly to Texas and then to Myrtle Beach and then back home, I can work an extra six days. This will more than pay for my flights."

She flew to Texas and I rode my motorcycle on a round-about route to Myrtle Beach. A week or so later, the four of us met at Ocean 22. Carol had injured her knee several weeks earlier and it was hard for her to walk so I had suggested we postpone our trip. I requested her to get an appointment to get her knee fixed, but she would not hear of it. We checked in on Saturday, October 15, 2016 for an expected eight-night stay. We lounged by the pool and on the beach, had fun dinners and generally a grand time. During our stay, Ed and I went golfing while Carol and Becky got manicures and pedicures. On Thursday we went to Moe Moon's for lunch and had plans to attend a movie that night, enjoy a river cruise the next day and a sneak in a few more activities before we would leave for home.

The movie never happened. The river cruise was cancelled. The worst nightmare one could ever imagine began. At 1:15 P.M., October 20, 2016, life changed forever. My high school sweetheart, as I had known her for over fifty years, left me.

My children suggested I set up a Caring Bridge page, to inform our friends and family of Carol's status. They weren't sure if I'd have the mental and emotional energy to respond to the countless emails and text messages. I was in a daze just trying to understand what was happening and Caring Bridge seemed like a logical thing to do. My girls helped me set it up and I wrote regular posts. I am sharing my words from that online journal, as well as private thoughts only made known to the closest of Carol's friends and family. In a few places I have included posts or letters from our children or other friends, but most of this is my words, my thoughts and my anguish. I have changed the names of a few individuals in this book out of respect for their privacy.

I don't remember how I informed my children, Stephanie, Mickolyn and Chad, that their mom's life was in a precarious and fragile state. As best I can remember, this is what transpired.

- 1:20 P.M. while on the way to the hospital, I text my kids, "Something happened to Mom at lunch. She kind of passed out at the restaurant. She is on her way to the hospital via ambulance right now."

- I didn't know if it was serious or not, thinking it was maybe just food poisoning.

- From the ER, I text them that it's very serious, but I didn't have any details.

- Chad called me, and I told him that if he didn't fly to Myrtle Beach immediately, Mom may not be alive when he got here.

- Mickolyn called wondering what was going on. She said she would come as soon as she could, but I told her that Mom may not be alive when she gets here.

- After the second message, Steph left work, went home and packed.

I don't remember talking to any of them. I don't remember sending a text message. I just remember sitting in a little room by myself with no tissues, just wondering what had just happened.

Day 1 The Beginning 10/20/2016

Carol and I were on a little fall vacation with our dear friends Ed and Becky in Myrtle Beach, SC. Thursday noon we ate lunch at a little restaurant on the boardwalk. We had just finished lunch and were just sitting there visiting when Carol complained of being really dizzy and nauseous. It soon became apparent that this was something very serious as she passed out. EMS arrived and took her to the hospital in

Myrtle Beach where she was diagnosed with a serious bleed in her cerebellum. Carol is on life support systems and under sedation. She has not regained consciousness since we left the restaurant. She is listed as stable, but very critical.

What just happened? One-minute Carol, Ed, Becky and I are enjoying lunch beside the beach and the next Carol is very sick. It all happened so quickly. She is dizzy, then begins to vomit. She says, "I think I need to go to the hospital, but I'm so dizzy I don't think I can walk," and she never speaks again. She's unconscious. There is another restaurant patron, a nurse, standing there trying to take Carol's vital signs and reporting them to the manager, who in turn is relaying them to the 911 operator. The paramedics and ambulance arrive in what seems like hours, but is really only minutes, and very quickly have her loaded on a gurney and are taking her away. One of the EMT's ask me for her license, tells us where they are taking Carol and they leave. Ed, Becky and I follow in their car and arrive at Grand Strand Emergency Room approximately 20 minutes later. When I arrive, I ask at the desk about Carol, but they have no record of her yet. The lady tells me to just have a seat and they will get me in a few minutes. An eternity passes, and I ask again about Carol's condition. The receptionist calls someone, turns back towards me and tells me to go over to the consultation room around the corner and wait for the doctor to come talk to me. This does not look good. I sit there all alone and wait. I can hear doors opening and closing and people going back and forth but no one comes into my little room. I peek out and motioned for Ed and Becky to join me. Finally, a doctor comes into the room, almost like you see on TV and explains about Carol's condition. She is alive. As I rode to the hospital and then sat in the little room, I feared she had already died. When they told me to go to the little room, I figured it was to tell me that they were sorry and that they had done all they could, but she had died. But she's alive, but in very critical condition. How can this be? We were just having lunch. We have plans for tonight and tomorrow and the rest of our lives. A few minutes later we were led to the Neuro Science Intensive Care Unit, NSICU, where Carol lies in a bed with all sorts of life support systems attached to her body and she was unconscious, but alive.

Bill

This entry was never posted. It was an email I sent to my children at 4:40 P.M. on 10/20/2016:

> Steph,
>
> Unless we hear that you got a rental car, Ed will leave MB around 8 eastern time to come to Charleston, SC to get you and bring you back to the hospital. You can either stay at the hospital or go back to the resort. We have a 2-bedroom until Monday. I will check on extending our stay if we need to.
>
> Chad and Mickolyn,
>
> One or both of you should reserve a rental car at Myrtle Beach airport. Ed and Becky will probably leave on Friday once you all are here. They were planning to leave on Saturday anyway, but once they leave we won't have a car. I rode my motorcycle out here.
>
> As for Mom. We had just finished lunch at this place on the boardwalk & Mom started feeling really dizzy. She said her head was just swimming. Then she started vomiting and just got worse and worse. I finally had a lady call EMS and they seemed to take forever to get there but it probably wasn't that long.
>
> Once at the ER they suspected a stroke. They drilled into the cerebellum and drained almost 50cc of blood immediately.

They have her scheduled for another CT scan at 8:00 tonight which should give more information on brain status and bleeding. Nurse said she is stable but very critical. Pupils are non-responsive and from what I can tell and from what they are saying, there doesn't seem to be much brain activity. But I might have totally misread this.

She is on life support systems which doesn't sound very good to me. I told the nurse that all three of you were coming and she said that was probably a good thing.

I hope and pray Mom is still alive when you get here but right now, I'm not sure if that will be the case. God can work miracles and I think she really needs one.

Love you all,
Dad

Day 2 Morning 10/21/2016

Our oldest daughter, Stephanie Hamell, arrived around 1:30 AM today. Our son, Chad Funnemark will arrive around 10:00 AM today and our middle daughter, Mickolyn Clapper will arrive around 11:00 AM today. At this point we have no real answers. We are just waiting on the doctors to evaluate her and give us some answers. She's in God's hands.

After the morning visit by the doctor we know a little more. Carol is stable, which I guess is a positive sign. They think the bleeding has stopped or nearly so, but she is still in very critical condition. The next few days will be critical. I'm sorry I don't have more information at this time. Stephanie and Chad are both here at the hospital with me and

Mickolyn is on the ground at the airport and will soon join us.

Bill

Day 2 Evening Journal entry by Bill Funnemark — 10/21/2016

Well here it is Friday evening and we are back in Carol's room. I know Carol and I would love to be back in Iowa watching Will Clapper and the rest of the CMB Raiders play football, but we are here instead. I am so glad the Stephanie, Mickolyn and Chad are here with me. We talked to the doctors earlier and there is no change. The best news is she has not changed. That may not seem like good news to most of you, but no change means she is not getting worse. It is hard to watch her just lying there wondering if she can hear us but not showing any response or very little. But there is more response to stimulus tonight than last night. Every little step is important but there is a really, long journey to go.

Love you Babe,
Bill

Day 3 Hope on Saturday morning Journal entry by Bill Funnemark — 10/22/2016

I am sitting on the 14th floor of the resort that Carol and I love, looking out at the ocean, tears flowing down my cheeks, trying to type and I am just overcome with awe. There is HOPE today. Mickolyn spent the night at the hospital while Chad, Steph and I spent the night in real beds for some much-needed sleep. Mickolyn text this morning that Carol showed some response to the nurse's stimuli. This is the first sign that of any conscious action on Carol's part since this whole thing started almost two days ago.

The many emails, texts and responses of love, support and prayers from all of you has been so special to all of us. I even had a message from a friend who played softball with me maybe 30 years ago. I didn't even recognize his name until he mentioned softball. I know God has a plan. I don't know what it is at this point, but I know he has a plan. I do know that Carol has a long road to recovery, but she is making small steps each day. I don't want anyone to think she is out of the woods yet though. Many things must happen, like being able to breathe on her own and many others.

I always knew Carol and I had a lot of friends, but you all are amazing. Some of you have been through similar tragic events and many of you have not. But I want each and every one of you to know just how much we appreciate you.

Figure 1 is a sunrise picture from our resort. This just gives me HOPE. Praise the Lord.

Figure 1 Sunrise on Myrtle Beach

Day 3 God is good in big and small matters. Journal entry by Stephanie Hamell — 10/22/2016

So we have plenty of time right now to sit and contemplate this situation, so many miracles have already happened, Mom's friend Becky sent me a list of her thoughts.

- there was a nurse at the restaurant who helped tend to my mom right away and gave important information to the 911 operator to relay to the crew en route to her.

- the ambulance had easy access to Mom, they had plans for the next day to be on a river cruise, that would have been catastrophic had this happened at that time.

- the hospital has on staff at all times a highly trained team of trauma doctors who knew exactly what had to be done within minutes of her arrival.

- her first nurse was a Christian woman who was praying her while treating her.

- with very short notice all of us kids were able to get flights to not the world's biggest airport and Mom and Dad's great friends Ed and Becky were able to be with Dad, help transport us and get us to the hospital. (there are almost NO cars available here due the recent hurricane and we miraculously got a car after all the websites said no cars available!)

The Bible tells us to give thanks in all things, we have so much to be thankful for at this time. All the things that God laid out before and during this crisis and the work he is continuing to do for my mom and us.

The nurse just said to my mom, "You're doing great girl, give us a thumbs-up Carol," and she did! Keep praying because it is working. Small steps forward are what we are thankful for right now. God is good, a verse that means a lot to me and has helped me is "Be Still and know that I am God."

Day 3 Blessed Journal entry by Bill Funnemark — 10/22/2016

Just a short note for right now. Carol is in Grand Strand Regional Medical Center in Myrtle Beach, South Carolina. Please do not send any flowers or cards or anything else here. For one, I don't think they allow flowers in the ICU. Second, we don't have a way to get all that stuff back home. I can only carry so much junk on my motorcycle! Your comments on Caring Bridge, Facebook, emails or personal messages are more than enough. We greatly appreciate all of them. If you feel you really need to send a card, send it to our home in Algona.

Many of you have offered your help with anything we may need. At this point, there is nothing we need. Carol's nephew Todd diligently checks our house and picks up our mail. The only thing at the moment I can think of that needs doing is raking my leaves. But it's too early. We have some maple trees in our back yard that don't drop their leaves until mid-November. But really, we are fine right now. Thanks to all of you.

Bill

Day 3 Saturday night Journal entry by Bill Funnemark — 10/22/2016

Carol continues to make little baby steps of progress. But when we talked to one of the doctors tonight we are reminded that she is a long way from being out of the woods. There are many issues yet to conquer. She has to be able to breathe on her own and eat and process food. We won't know for a few days how her systems are working and if she can carry on normal life functions. We are just reminded to be patient and trust in God's plan. Go Cubs!!!

Day 4 Sunday morning: Praise God Journal entry by Bill Funnemark — 10/23/2016

Just a short note of praise. Steph and I are in the hospital with Carol, while Mickolyn and Chad are back at the resort showering. I just started reading comments and came across this one from Steph's friend Lori, "We continue to pray for Carol and ask that God heal her body and mind. We pray for that glorious day when she opens her eyes to see her family by her side. We are thankful that for the Lord!! And Chicago was rocking last night with a Cubs win!!!" Well not more than 30 seconds after we read this she opened her eyes a little. Praise God.

She is a long way from being out of the woods, but she continues to make small, little steps forward. The next 24-48 hours are critical as they try to determine if she can breathe on her own and if her digestive system works. So far all signs are going in a positive direction but we also know she is still just beginning her marathon. As many of you know I run marathons, not fast but I run them. Well in Carol's case on her 26.2 mile journey to recovery, I think she is still on mile one. She has a long way to go and she has some steep hills to climb before she can get past mile two or three. But she has God and hundreds of friends and people who have never met her on, her side. Thank you everyone for your prayers and offers of help. I can't answer all the emails or reply to all the comments, but I will do the best I can. We read them all and so appreciate them.

Bill

Day 4 Sunday Evening Journal entry by Bill Funnemark — 10/23/2016

It has been a slow day for all of us. I think Carol made it into the 2nd mile of her marathon but it's up a pretty good hill. At times, she has responded to our stimuli, moved her fingers a little, opened her eyes a little bit but nothing major. There are a few signs that her digestive system is working a little but they are proceeding very slowly with this. For those of you who have never gone through anything like this, it is really hard to imagine how slow this whole process is. It is hard to be patient. When Carol opened her eyes a little earlier today, I wanted to just wake her up. She can't speak of course because she has tubes going down her throat and esophagus. But I want her to just open her eyes and speak to me or at least smile. But we just have to wait.

It has been such a blessing to have Stephanie, Mickolyn and Chad here with me. I can stay as long as I need to but they each have families and jobs, so I really appreciate them being here. Many of you have offered all kinds of services and we truly do appreciate each and every one. Thanks to those of you who bringing meals to my kids' families. I hope no one is bringing food to my house, because I won't be around to enjoy them anytime soon.

Again, thank you for your prayers and kind words. My Corwith-Wesley-LuVerne CWL) family will always hold a special place in my heart and we have heard from so many of you, it's amazing. Carol has made so many friends through her work at Good Samaritan Care Center and now through her nurse consulting work along with all our other friends that there are literally hundreds or maybe thousands of people praying for her and us. All I can say is thank you, thank you, thank you.

One thing I do wish though, is that kids would update this journal too. Those of you who know me well, know how I dislike writing a journal.

I used to have to do this once in a while in education and I always dreaded it. I guess we all have to make sacrifices. LOL. Since Chad is leaving in the morning, we all decided to go down to the beach for a family picture. Figure 2 taken at our resort. Wish you could be in it too Mom.

Figure 2 Chad, Mickolyn, Stephanie and Bill at the beach.

Bill

Day 5 Monday afternoon Journal entry by Bill Funnemark — 10/24/2016

This has been a busy day for all of us except Carol. She's just chilling. Chad had to go home today, so this morning was quite emotional for all us. Stephanie and Mickolyn are planning to stay a few more days. When Carol and I originally planned this trip, we had rented a two-bedroom unit at Ocean 22 Hilton Grand Vacations in Myrtle Beach for eight nights and were going to be joined by Ed and Becky. They left on Friday which gave us space for the three kids and me. Our time was up this morning but Hilton had another unit, not ocean front, just ocean view. So with switching rooms, taking Chad to the airport and switching rental cars, it was a busy morning. When Steph and Chad arrived, there were no rental cars available at either Charleston or Myrtle Beach airports due to the hurricane. When Mickolyn arrived at Myrtle Beach last Friday morning there were only a couple cars available. This morning we took that one back and got a cheaper one but actually turned out to be a bigger one.

Carol has continued to make slow progress and we become more enlightened about the whole process. We learned that the sedative she was receiving the first few days in an attempt to keep her calm and give her brain time to repair itself is absorbed into fat tissue. Fat tissue is for long term storage and thus takes longer to be metabolized and its effects reduced. This is why she was a little less responsive yesterday than the day before. At least that's part of the explanation we think. We're not sure where she stands right now but we think she is improving. My guess she is still on mile two, still running up a steep hill, but nearing mile three. The critical moment will be moving her off the breathing tube which will be in a day or so.

Bill

Day 6 Tuesday morning (I think) Journal entry by Bill Funnemark — 10/25/2016

It was my turn to spend the night at the hospital with Carol. Steph, Mickolyn and Chad each took their turns and last night it was my time again. This recliner is no Craftmatic or Sleep Number bed for sure. After a while I just decided to get up, brush my teeth, get a cup of coffee and catch up on emails etc. Sometime during the night, I got an email letting me know that Chad had made it safely back home to Oregon. I'm sure his girls will be happy to see him this morning. I know we all, Carol included, were so happy that he could make the trip across the country to be with us. Stephanie and Mickolyn are still here for a few more days anyway.

There is not much to report about Carol. They just took her for another CT scan so they can compare to the scan from a few days ago. She had a peaceful night and as far as I know, nothing negative happened. I don't know if there were any positive steps or not. Progress is so slow that it is hard for me to see any change. I'm not saying there isn't change, but it is hard to see it since we are here so much.

It is easy when you are in a situation like we're in right now, to think the whole world revolves around you and your problems. But life goes on. As I was checking updates from various sources I came across a post about Mike and the fact that he had a farm accident. I had some of Mike's family as students at CWL High School and I am indirectly related to part of his family. My heart goes out to all of his family as they deal with their own hardships.

Bill

Day 6 Tuesday afternoon Journal entry by Bill Funnemark — 10/25/2016

Not much has happened with Carol today. She is holding her own, but there have been no big steps forward or backwards. We have talked to several staff members from the hospital on various topics and the message we keep getting is to be patient, brain injuries take a long time to heal. We don't want to wait a long time. We want to hear that Carol will wake up tomorrow and be fine but that just isn't going to happen. So we mostly just sit and wait for God's plan to unfold. It's not our plan but God's plan. We don't know what it is right now but we know it's out of our hands.

On another note. I had my bike parked at the resort we are staying at for several days and then a couple days ago I rode it to the hospital. The rear tire was a little low, so I pumped it up. No big deal. My bike sat in the hospital parking lot for a couple days and this morning I decided to ride it back to the resort and the rear tire was a little low again. When I got back to the parking garage I decided to investigate and discovered there is a small nail in the tire. I plugged it but it still leaked. So I tried another plug and still leaks. I really didn't need this right now, but I will take care of it. I have plenty of time.

Let's go Cubs!!!

Day 6 Thoughts on a plane. Journal entry by Chad Funnemark — 10/25/2016

So, there have been a couple updates from my dad since I left yesterday. I had plenty of time on the airplane to think, and I put some of thoughts down. The following was written Monday evening, so please keep that in mind.

As I'm sure a lot of you might know, I'm not much for sharing my feelings, especially with the public, but my dad has asked that my sisters and I add to the Caring Bridge for my mom. I'm doing this once for him because I think it is probably helpful (to me, Mickolyn, Stephanie, and my dad).

On Thursday, I got a text from my Dad that my mom was sick and taking an ambulance to the hospital. I was concerned, but not overly concerned, she's only 68, and seems to be really enjoying her retirement. She's not stressed like she was at the Good Sam. But, quickly, I found out things were a lot worse than I initially thought.

I got on the first flight from Portland to Myrtle Beach, SC. I got on a plane Thursday night, hoping that my mom would still be alive when I landed. At this point, I didn't know if that was a real possibility or not. Based on what my dad was hearing, there was a good chance I wouldn't make it in time. I flew overnight and got to the hospital on Friday around noon. I have seen and experienced a lot in my life (or at least, I thought so), but nothing can prepare you for seeing your mom intubated on a hospital bed in a neuro-ICU. Strong, steady Chad went out the window quickly. Pure fear and sadness is the best way I can describe what I felt.

I'm sure if you're reading this, you've seen the updates from my dad for the last couple of days, so I don't need to go hour by hour, but there have been ups and downs and lots of what the hell is going on. My mom was very unresponsive, sometimes it seemed like she was maybe squeezing a hand, but is that wishful thinking?? It sort of reminded me as a kid fishing at Smith Lake. We would have a bobber and with every little wave, it seemed like maybe my bobber went under water. My dad would say, I don't think so, but reel it in if you want. Usually, I still had a worm on my hook, and so, I'd cast it back out. Anyone who knows me now, might know that I can patiently fish for hours and not catch anything. Waiting for my mom, takes patience to a different level. Maybe like waiting for Santa as a kid, but eventually, Santa showed up because you would fall asleep. I guess what I'm trying to say, is that waiting for someone with the brain injury like my mom had is the hardest thing I've ever experienced. It seems like hours and hours of waiting for her to maybe move her eyebrow a ¼ of an inch. Pure hell!

What else can I say about what is going on? Not sure because I'm on a plane flying home to my family. I miss Laura and my girls so much. Growing up, your parents give you the peace you need when you're scared or hurt. I still look towards my parents for support, but that role has shifted to Laura. I don't just miss her, but I need her. She hasn't had to say much to me in the last few days, but what she has provided is the support that I needed. She always seems to know exactly what I need in the moment. She can shelve her needs in moments like this, and be there for me. Thank you for that!

What is going on with my mom? I don't know! When I left the hospital today, I had no idea if that is the last time I'll see my mom or not. I truly hope and feel it wasn't goodbye. I know that God can work miracles and talking to the hospital staff, it seems my mom has already been a miracle. The nurse who was there Thursday when my mom got to the hospital was surprised to see her today! To me, that is a miracle. Granted, she's not carrying on conversations or anything yet, but she's still fighting!

I really don't know what is going to happen in the next few days, weeks or months. Will my mom be back to herself? I sure hope so! She has my dad, my sisters and me, and nine grandkids who need her. My girls need her to take them to Yogurt Shack and get too many sweets on their ice cream. Who's going to bring us puppy chow from The Chocolate Season? They need someone who is going to spoil them whenever she's around! Laura needs her too. Laura needs a supportive mother-in-law. They have really grown close over the years, and I'm sure they will continue to grow even closer. And, I need her too. I need someone who is going to be there like only a mom can be. I need to be able get the very random voice to text that makes no sense other than, me knowing my mom is reaching out. I need my mom to be around longer. Maybe I'm being selfish, but I'm not ready to say goodbye yet. She has a lot she needs to experience! She needs to experience her other eight grandkids graduate high school; she needs to experience her grandkids getting married if they want to; the list goes on and on. It's not her time!! Basically, I'm not ready to let my mom go yet, and I don't think anyone else is either!

My mom is an amazing person. Ask the hundreds of families from Good Sam she's supported over the years. She put everyone else first for so long, and now, she needs your support. We need your support. I am on my way home to my family, and my sisters will follow suit in a few days. But, my dad will be staying in a hospital room with my mom. They have known each other since grade school. They were high school sweethearts. They've been married for 46 years. Please take a minute to think about how sad it would be to lose your best friend. Now, think of that and to be 1,500 miles from home and alone, too. Please take a minute today/tonight to think about my dad. He's done a lot for people and he's not one to ask for help. So, I will for him. If you can help him out, please do so. Please, if you can rake some leaves, see if their yard needs mowed, take a minute to send him an email, it would be greatly appreciated by all of us. He'll try to respond, I'm sure. He has lots of time on his hands right now. But, this is going to go on for a long time. Please do me a favor and put a calendar entry in your phone to email my dad in a week or 10 days. I know many of you have experienced pains like this too, and have your own lives going on, but if possible, please don't forget about what we are going through and give support if you can.

Thanks for all your support. I appreciate it. No matter what happens, we'll be OK. However, we won't be the same. This has changed us forever. Do me a favor and reach out to your family and loved ones and just say hi. This just reminds us of how precious life is, and how quickly it can change. My mom was eating lunch, and 10 minutes later, she was in an ICU and hasn't woken up. Life can change in an instant.

I want to thank everyone that has reached out to me personally. I haven't gotten back to many of you. I hope you understand. God can work miracles and I'm praying for one. Thanks for everything.

Chad

PS I thought this song maybe seemed appropriate too: "Fight Song" by Rachel Platten

Day 7 Wednesday Morning Journal entry by Bill Funnemark — 10/26/2016

I spent Monday night at the hospital with Carol while the girls went back to our condo. So yesterday was a long day for me along with everyone else here. Carol has been stable the last couple days. The nurses and doctors keep telling us she is making progress, but it is hard for me to see that she is moving forward. I guess since I am so close I just can't see much change but when a nurse who hasn't been on duty for a couple days comes back in he/she is pleasantly surprised at her progress. We watched Monday night football here at the hospital but since the game didn't involve any of our favorite teams Carol didn't really get into it. But last night we watched the Cubs game and I'm sure she was listening and was probably very disappointed in their performance. Everyone tells us she can hear us whether she responds or not, she can still hear us. So maybe she could actually hear the baseball game.

Sometime today Carol will have what they call a "Trach & Peg" performed. This procedure involves removing the breathing and feeding tubes that currently go in through her mouth and then replacing them with a tracheotomy and a tube directly into her stomach. They assured us that they wouldn't even consider this procedure if they didn't think there was any hope. So we take this as a sign that the doctors see she is making progress and there is hope for long term recovery. In the mean time we just wait.

Many of you have wanted to know how you can help or is there anything you can do for us. Some have offered help with housing and some of you have offered other help. Thanks for each and every offer. We have housing in Myrtle Beach secured through November 4th if in fact we are here that long. Yesterday there was talk of moving Carol to a specialized rehab center somewhere in the southeastern US. We don't know when or where this might be, but that will probably be the next step when she is ready for a different type of care. Sometime down the road we will be coming back to Iowa, but she is not able to be transferred that far just yet. We'll worry about all those details when the time comes.

I guess she maybe finished mile two and is still going up the hill on mile three. That's about all for now.

Bill

Day 7 Wednesday Afternoon Journal entry by Bill Funnemark — 10/26/2016

This post has nothing much to offer for updates on Carol. So, if that's what you are looking for, too bad. I just wanted to say thank you to everyone who has commented on Caring Bridge and to us directly through Facebook, email, text or messenger. I hope no one is trying to contact me on my Twitter account because although I actually have an account, I have no idea how to check it. It was just one of those things that my students help me setup one day because they thought I needed it. So far, I have survived without it and that's how it will continue.

Some of you, Mary Lee and Liz, (you know who you are) must not have a life and just sit by your computer waiting for my next update. So for you two special friends and many others, this update is just for you. LOL

Although this whole situation just really sucks, I can't cry and feel sorry for myself all day long. I have many moments when I feel down, but then a little bit later I will forget about our current situation and think about fun times. So let me just share a few random fun thoughts about life in general.

Some of you might wonder why I'm here with my motorcycle and Carol flew here. The simple answer is because that's the way Carol wants it. Several years ago, while both Carol and I were working we had very different vacation schedules. I, as a teacher, had most of my summers off while Carol was the Director of Nursing at Good Samaritan Care Center. She would take a week or so of vacation to go visit grandkids throughout the year, but I couldn't do that. So, when summer came she didn't want to waste her vacation getting there and would fly to Oregon to visit Chad in Oregon while I'd ride my motorcycle. A win-win. Carol knows how much I love to ride and she encourages me to take the scenic route and enjoy the trip as well as the visit with family. I think she got spoiled getting to fly places rather than spending 12 hours a day on the back of my bike. Now that we're retired we have the time to take the scenic route, but she still flies. Somehow being retired to Carol is different than it is for me. She works as a nurse consultant, visiting many long-term care centers in Iowa sharing her expertise. She loves her new job and now doesn't want to waste time driving or riding to family or vacation spots. So again, she flies; I ride. A win-win. So that's why I'm here on my bike.

OK. That's all for now. I hope you get your afternoon fix Mary Lee. And for those of you who know how I love journaling, you know what a sacrifice this is. Seriously, it is therapeutic for me. It gives me something to do. The TV channels in the hospital suck. No old westerns or other old reruns that I love. But it's probably just as well. It drives Carol crazy to have to sit and watch two hours straight of Newhart or Andy Griffith.

Bill

Day 7 Afternoon surprise Journal entry by Bill Funnemark — 10/26/2016

Thanks Jim, Patti, Cassie and Alesha.

Day 7 No Surgery Yet Journal entry by Bill Funnemark — 10/26/2016

Carol was supposed to have a surgical procedure today but since this was not deemed critical, they will do it in when they can. We thought it would be this morning or afternoon, but it still hasn't happened. There have been several emergencies not related to Carol, that took priority. We'll send an update after her surgery.

Bill

Day 8 Thursday morning. Is it Thursday? Journal entry by Stephanie Hamell — 10/27/2016

I'm awake early because it was my night to sleep at the hospital, as you might imagine, sleeping in a recliner on an ICU wing is not the best sleep you'll ever have, but if sleeping here means my mom is still here, I'm happy to do it. My dad will update on the trach and peg procedure my mom had last night.

When this whole thing happened, and we were left with sitting in the hospital room scared and waiting, waiting for what? We didn't know, couldn't really even let our heads go there. We "needed" something. We sort of fell into roles, Dad-social media and correspondence, Steph-took on my mom's usual role of prayer warrior and emotional support, Mickolyn-asking hard questions and holding the medical staff accountable, Chad-comic relief and voice of reason when we needed it. We cobbled together a little existence and for the moment, it's working.

I'm looking at Mom right now thinking what a week she's had. The docs said with her medical history, the fact that she had this hemorrhagic stroke was really just a case of bad luck. I'll say. She has been drilled, hair clipped, poked, intubated, had surgery, monitored and possibly hardest of all for her, hasn't had Diet Dew in a week. She keeps showing up, if you know anything about my mom, you know she shows up. She is strong like no one I know, she goes about the business of getting stuff done. Right now, she is fighting her way back, each day there are little challenges and big challenges, but she keeps showing up, she knows we're here and we need her. That's how my mom rolls.

We can't thank everyone enough for all the well wishes and most of all the prayers. The medical staff here have told us on a few occasions that she's in miracle territory. If you have ever spent time on this kind of ICU, you know they don't blow sunshine. They tell you the truth, they told my dad Thursday afternoon, "Most people in your wife's condition don't survive, get your kids here." She's still here and making steps, truly all of the praise and glory go to God, he really is a God of miracles. We have so much to be thankful for and I can't believe how truly blessed we are. The days are long, and it seems nothing is happening, but things are happening behind the scenes in my mom's brain. She's still fighting, she's still showing up so we're going to do the same.

Thanks to our spouses and family back home for pulling double duty so we can be here. Thanks also to all of friends back home taking care of our families with meals, and gift cards, and rides, etc. Thanks to friends back home for the gift cards and treats we have received here. Thank you for the messages and most of all the prayers. It means so much, and honestly, I believe that's why Mom is still here making progress. So, we wait and are reminded to "Be Still and know that I am God."

Have a great day.

Steph on behalf of Dad, Mickolyn, and Chad.

Day 8 Thursday morning Journal entry by Bill Funnemark — 10/27/2016

Good morning world. Praise the Lord for small steps. We waited all day and finally last night the surgeons did her trach and peg, which we think is a big step forward. Carol is still on a ventilator, but now there are no tubes in her mouth or down her trachea and esophagus. This morning she looks better, her hands are not as swollen, and it is wonderful to actually be able to see her face instead all the tubes etc. When the nurse came in to check her shortly after I arrived, Carol did respond a little. Her eyes could sort of track and she held them open for a little bit. Don't overreact. It's not like she followed me around the room or anything but there was a little eye movement and she did respond to some other stimuli.

So where are we mile wise? It is really hard to say, but I think we are nearing the top of the three-mile long hill. Once we reach the top there will a long journey. This is definitely a marathon or maybe even an ultra-marathon.

A special thanks to everyone at First Baptist Church (Grace Church) of Algona for all your support and a special thanks to Pastor Peter and

Pastor Patrick and the Elder Board. Sorry but it will always be First Baptist to me.

This morning before Mickolyn and I went back to the hospital we walked down toward the beach. Carol and I love going to the ocean and Figure 3 is Mickolyn and me in front of our resort just waiting for the time when Carol will be standing here beside me. Figure 4 is me holding Carol's hands and Figure 5 is Mickolyn. We didn't want anyone to see her head because she would be horrified for anyone to see her hair or what's left of it. Alecia (sorry about the spelling) from Innovations, you will have your work cut out for you! LOL

Carol is by no means out of the woods yet, but today we all just seem so encouraged by the miracles God has done so far. I don't know what the next few days or the next month will bring, but today we are feeling better. Tonight might be different but this morning we are all smiles. Thanks for all your continued prayers and support.

Bill

Figure 3 Mickolyn and Bill

Figure 4 Bill and hands.

Figure 5 Mickolyn and hands

Day 8 Thursday night Journal entry by Bill Funnemark — 10/27/2016

Just a short note. I took the afternoon off and had some me time. I took a short motorcycle ride, went for a run and had a virgin Pina colada down by the beach. Then Stephanie, Mickolyn and I went out for a nice dinner thanks to some great friends who sent us a gift card. I'm back at the hospital and the girls are back at the condo. Carol is just hanging in there. I would love to report that she had a wonderful day and made tremendous progress but that just didn't happen. Again, the staff keeps telling us to be patient, it's a long, slow process.

As I sit here checking Facebook and other sources, I am reminded that we aren't the only family who are facing a crisis. Mike is in a hospital with severely broken leg and knee. His girls were my students at CWL. Heal quickly Mike. Then there is Tricia who has a little girl with some serious medical issues. My heart goes out to both families. I know they are praying for us just like I am praying for them.

Not much more to report tonight.

Bill

Day 9 Friday Morning Journal entry by Bill Funnemark — 10/28/2016

I guess it's Friday morning but it seems like just another morning. Carol had a peaceful, uneventful night, but unfortunately there is no change in her condition. They took her for another CT scan early this morning to see if there is any internal change, but I have not heard back with any results yet.

It was my turn to spend the night with Carol at the hospital. We have been on a rotation with each family member taking a turn. For those of you who have never spent a night in a hospital room, let me tell you that it is not best place to sleep. There are all kinds of noises, people coming in and out of the room and a not so comfy chair to sleep on. But I'm not complaining, I'm just a little tired.

The pulmonary team just came and turned off her ventilator to see if Carol can breathe on her own. So far she is doing it. This is a huge step. The ventilator is still in place as a backup, but she will be on her own for a few hours. The doctor said she was doing great. The CT scan showed less brain swelling so things are progressing inside her head too.

Praise the Lord for every step she takes. I would say that she is maybe at the top of that miserably long hill and has now reached a point where she just needs to keep making small steps forward. I would say she's starting mile four. But again, we are reminded she has a long way to go, but we certainly are encouraged by these positive steps.

Bill

Day 9 Friday Evening Journal entry by Bill Funnemark — 10/28/2016

It's not a good sign when you start typing and the autocomplete already has Friday Evening in the memory. It is hard to believe our ordeal began over a week ago. Everyone at Grand Strand Medical Center has been great, but they keep telling us this will be a slow process and there will be many ups and downs. And they sure are right about that. Some of the staff were surprised that they did the trach and peg so early, because usually it's anywhere from 10 to 20 days before the patient is ready. But Carol had it done on day six. Normally when they turn off the ventilator it's only for three-four hours and then gradually extend it each day as the body responds. Carol was off the machine for nearly 10 hours today. The only reason they turned it back on was to give her time to rest tonight. This was a big step forward. But to bring us back to reality, she was very unresponsive to commands or touch. I don't know what this all means, but like the doctors keep saying forward progress followed by back tracking. So we just keep hanging in there one day at a time looking for anything positive we can grasp.

On another note, since life does go on outside the hospital. I think I mentioned or maybe not that I had a flat tire on my bike. I picked up a nail someplace, probably here in Myrtle Beach. I tried to plug it and the first plug didn't work. So I tried a second one and it still leaked a little. So I added some tire snot and that seems to be holding, maybe. But since I have a wheel and tire warranty on my bike, it won't cost me anything to replace the tire. I contacted a local dealer (non-Triumph since there aren't any here) and they actually had my tire size in stock. We took the bike there this morning and hopefully I will get it back tomorrow. I'm not sure how I will get it back to Iowa yet, but I'll figure something out.

Carol's oldest sister Barb, who lives in Johnston, Iowa, and her daughter Ann, who lives in Indiana, are going to drive Carol's car out to Myrtle Beach and spend some time with me since our two girls are both going back home to their own families. I will have a car here which will be a little more convenient than my bike. Carol will eventually be transferred to a rehab center, but we have no idea when or where that will be. Having a car will be useful. If any of you want to take a late fall motorcycle trip, I could set you up with a one-way trip back to Iowa!!

Go Cubs!!!

Bill

Day 10 Saturday Morning Journal entry by Bill Funnemark — 10/29/2016

Praise God we are still here at Grand Strand Medical Center in Myrtle Beach, South Carolina. No, we are not in Florida as some of you think. I say praise God because this means Carol is still with us and is at one of the best neurotrauma centers in the entire southeastern US. Although she has not been responding much to stimuli the last couple days, she is still making real progress. Yesterday she spent nine or 10 hours breathing on her own with no assistance from the breathing machine. Now again this morning she is breathing on her own. The top neurosurgeon, we call him Dr. Clint Eastwood because of his personality, keeps telling us things will wax and wane, wax and wane. The other day some of the staff said Carol was in the miracle group but I don't think our kids fully grasp the meaning of this. This morning our nurse flat out told Steph that probably over 90% of the patients who come in like Carol do not survive the first 24 hours. They are amazed at her progress. We have no basis for comparison since this is our first go around with brain trauma. But these people see it every day. God is good.

A group of ladies from Corwith sent Carol a prayer shawl and we decided we best take a picture of it to show it off. Figure 6 also shows Carol's freshly painted nails. Last week, seems like an eternity ago, Ed and I went golfing and Carol and Becky went and had their nails done. I think Ed and I had the better half of the deal.

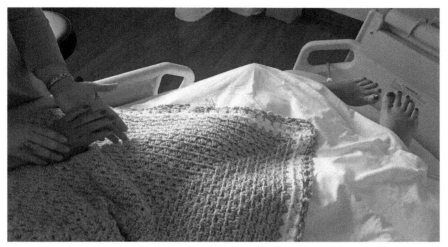
Figure 6 Prayer shawl

I got sidetracked from writing my update but I'm back now to finish up. Carol is a fighter and will continue to fight as long as she needs to. So many of you are praying for all us and that has to help.

So many of you have offered help and we all really appreciate the offers. I just want everyone to know we are doing fine right now. Some of you have taken meals to our children's homes, which is greatly appreciated by all, especially our grandchildren. I hope no one is taking meals to my home, because the only one home are the deer and I don't think they eat casseroles. But if you feel you really want to help, I think the best way is to contact me through Facebook messenger and we can make arrangements. But I want everyone to know that we are not soliciting help. Please do not feel like you have to do anything.

I think we are somewhere on mile four and just plodding along.

Bill

Day 10 Saturday night Journal entry by Bill Funnemark — 10/29/2016

Just a short note for tonight. A big thank you to Steve and Bobbie for bringing us dinner tonight. It was much appreciated. Thanks to the A Team from Texas for gift card at Bonefish Grill. A couple others gave us gift cards for dinners, but I think I already thanked you. A big thank you to Carl and your dad for raking some of my leaves today. Hopefully you left a few for friends from our church to rake too.

Tonight is sort of a melancholy evening. We went back to our condo to eat some dinner, but before we ate we went down to the beach for a little bit. The beach just isn't the same without my bride beside me. We all look forward to the day when she will be back beside me enjoying God's beauty. Mickolyn is leaving in the morning and it will be hard to see her go but it's just time for her to go back to her own family and her job. Steph is planning to leave on Tuesday for the same reasons.

OK, enough sad thoughts for tonight. We were watching random football games thinking no way would the Iowa State game be broadcast. But to our surprise it was on. So we got to watch the last five minutes of the game. And in typical Cyclone form they came close but no cigar. Come on Cubs let's get a win tonight so the sports day won't be a total bust.

Nothing really to report on Carol's progress.

Bill

Day 11 Sunday morning 2 Journal entry by Bill Funnemark — 10/30/2016

This is the second Sunday morning I've spent in the NSICU and it sounds like it won't be the last. Carol is resting comfortably, breathing pretty much on her own but still in a coma. Doctors have Carol connected to the ventilator, but she is doing most of the work of breathing. Today they plan to completely remove her from the ventilator for a couple hours, so they can evaluate her ability to breathe totally on her own. The muscles involved in breathing are weak from lack of use just like any other muscle in your body and so they need to slowly recondition her body to handle this. So far, she is responding great to these trials. All of Carol's vital signs are good and things seem to be progressing in the right direction but at a slow pace. She is still in a coma and staff here tell us that this is not uncommon. We just need to be patient. Although no one knows for sure, I anticipate Carol being in NSICU for at least another week. But it could be less or a lot more. It just depends on how her body heals.

This morning our daughter Mickolyn is going home. This is a really tough time for all of us. I know she wants to stay longer but she also has a family of her own and a job. Thank you to all of the Baxter area friends who have been so generous to her family in her absence. Our oldest daughter Stephanie will be here a couple more days.

We are all hanging in there and are so thankful for every little step of progress Carol makes. We know God is in control and we just have to trust in His power. Thank you to everyone who has been praying for us and for all the kind deeds.

Bill

Day 12 Monday Morning 2 Journal entry by Bill Funnemark — 10/31/2016

Well it's Monday morning, well, actually afternoon, in Myrtle Beach, and we are still waiting for Carol to wake up. Yesterday we saw some more steps forward. Carol is not showing any signs of waking up anytime soon, but it will happen one of these days. But she has been totally breathing on her own without the aid of any machine. She did this most of the day yesterday and then they put her back on the ventilator for the evening to let her rest. But now this morning she is on her own again. There are of course sensors still connected to her in case something goes wrong, but this is a major step forward. We all are very impatient waiting for to wake up, but the staff here keeps telling us to not be in a hurry. The breathing on her own may actually slow down the awakening process because it is a strain on her body and probably her brain as she builds up her muscles again.

This morning shortly after we arrived at the hospital we received and basket full of health food, chips, sunflower seeds, root beer, beef jerky and maybe some other stuff. This is the kind of stuff a person needs to watch sports on TV. Carol won't be able to have any of it, but I sure can. We don't know who sent it other than our friends from Iowa. You know who you are though. Thank you so much whoever it was.

I know some of you want to send gift cards for food and gas etc. and we really appreciate it. If you are so inclined to do so, an eCard is probably the easiest, sent to my email address. But if you are technology challenged like so many of our friends my age, sending a physical card might be easier. Message me through Facebook or send me an email and I will send you instructions.

As I mentioned earlier, if you have to be stuck in this situation, being stuck in Myrtle Beach, SC isn't all that bad. This morning as Steph and I were walking into the hospital I remarked that it is a little strange that I need a sweatshirt to wear inside the hospital when it is so darn nice outside. They like to keep this place cold for sure. Carol's sister Barb and her daughter Ann are arriving tonight, and Stephanie will be leaving in the morning. So I am not alone and won't be for the near future.

What mile is Carol on today? I really don't know. She is still at the beginning of her marathon journey, maybe still on four. We just don't know how long this will take so we don't know where she is.

Bill

Day 13 Tuesday Morning 2 Journal entry by Bill Funnemark — 11/1/2016

Another absolutely beautiful morning in Myrtle Beach, SC and I'm sitting in an empty hospital room. I got here about 10:30 this morning and the staff was just getting Carol ready to go have an MRI done. So I'm just chillin' in her room. Stephanie spent the night with Carol, had a tearful good-bye and then I brought her back to the resort to pack. She left for the airport around 9:00 and hopes to get home to Texas this afternoon. Carol's sister Barb and her daughter Ann arrived last night and had a chance to spend some time with Carol before going back to the condo for the night. Those two ladies are out doing some grocery shopping and I'm here at the hospital catching up on my writing assignments.

Carol has done a great job of breathing on her own and all her vital signs are right in the normal range. Our biggest concern however is the lack of response to stimuli. The doctors and nurses all keep telling us that this is normal, but we sense there is some concern on their part as well as ours. As a consequence, this morning Carol is having an MRI done to get a better picture of her brain and try to be able to figure out what's going on in there, what kind of damage there might be and get a better idea of what to expect in the next few days and weeks.

As you can imagine there is a steady stream of texts between our three children and me, especially since all three have left or are leaving Myrtle

Beach. This morning on her way to work Mickolyn listened to the song "Glorious Unfolding" by Steven Curtis Chapman. I had never heard the song. So after they wheeled Carol out of the room to take her for her MRI I thought I'd give it a listen or even better watch the video. I just want to forewarn you to grab some tissues and go to a quiet place before you watch or listen to it.

Bill

Day 14 Wednesday Morning 2 Journal entry by Bill Funnemark — 11/2/2016

Time for my daily update. I don't have much to report this morning. Carol had an MRI yesterday and that showed nothing really new, just gave a clearer picture of her brain and confirmed what the doctors have already told us. She has a slightly elevated white count which would indicate an infection of some type and so she is on some type of antibiotic. The lab will continue to grow cultures in order to determine exactly what the infectious agent is so they can give her a more precise antibiotic. Her vitals remain strong but she remains unresponsive to voice or touch. So we just continue to wait for something to happen as her brain slowly goes through the healing process. She has an excellent staff in her corner but her progress remains in God's hands.

As far as my marathon analogy, I have no idea what mile she's on. I just know she's out there somewhere plodding along with the finish line nowhere in sight. Those of you who have ever run a marathon or something similar know the feeling. You are out there following along a trail, not really knowing where you are, just hoping you will finish. I think that's where I am this morning. Somewhere between mile five and mile 24. Because once you get to 24 you can almost smell the finish line 2.2 miles away and I don't smell anything yet. At least the ocean is beautiful and the view from the 14th floor of our condo is spectacular. And we're still hanging in there.

Day 14 stuck between two worlds Journal entry by Stephanie Hamell — 11/2/2016

I tearfully left MB this morning. It was gut wrenching saying goodbye for now to my mom. I slept at the hospital. I was able to spend a lot of the night quietly holding my mom's hand and talking to her. I'm so happy I had that quiet time with her...after all the goodbyes I just want to get home to Texas. Unfortunately I'm having trouble getting on a flight so I'm in Charlotte, NC wishing I was somewhere else. God alone knows the plans he has for my mom. With any luck I'll be home with Pete and my sweet boys tonight.

Day 15 Journal entry by Bill Funnemark — 11/3/2016

In about two hours it will have been a full 14 days since Carol's whole world changed and along with it so did everyone else's in our family. I stayed up very late last night to watch the Cubs win the World Series and so today we are all a little slow to get started. But Barb, Ann and I are beside Carol's bed just waiting and praying for something to happen. On the positive side, she has been breathing on her own since yesterday morning. Carol was running a fever and had some type of infection, but no fever today or yesterday and the antibiotic she is on seems to be working as her white count continues to move towards normal. All her vital signs are good. Now if she would please just wake up. She continues to be unresponsive to stimuli which is a big concern, but we are still hopeful that this will return soon.

As for me, I took a day off from my early morning workout. This eastern time zone thing is for the birds, especially if you stay up until 1:30

AM to watch a baseball game. Our sweet niece Ann is heading back to Indiana later today which means it will be just sister-in-law Barb and me holding down the fort. One of the nice things about having these two ladies here is that they can cook. One night we had pot roast with all the stuff that goes with it and last night pork chops. It sure beats going to a restaurant every night. Our condo has a full kitchen and I can cook but somehow cooking a frozen pizza just doesn't quite matchup with an actual home cooked meal. Thanks ladies.

On another note. As some of you know Carol has been a Longaberger consultant for many years. I know she has some fairly regular customers and does a show for you every so often. I on the other hand have no idea if you have placed an order lately and are waiting on a basket or other stuff. I personally don't see how any of you could possibly need any more baskets, but then that's a guy talking and I really don't understand these things. One of Carol's friends is going to go through some boxes that have come to our house recently in an effort to track down who the orders belong to. It would be helpful to know if any of you have placed an order anytime recently and are expecting something. If you are, please call, text or email me and I will help from this end to get you your baskets.

That's about all for today. Congratulations Cubs and let's go Cyclones tonight.

Bill

Day 16 Journal entry by Bill Funnemark — 11/4/2016

Has it really been over two weeks now since this nightmare began? Yes it has. What has happened in these two weeks? The Cyclones lost another football game, although they did have the lead for about nine seconds. The Vikings got beat by the Bears. The Cubs won a few post season baseball games. Our grandson Will Clapper was named 1st team all-district offensive lineman as a sophomore. A former CWL student Carl (not her real name) and her dad came and raked my leaves. Ed and Becky went home and now are in Arizona. I've seen all three of our children together for the first time in a long time. Not the best reason for a family get together but it was great to have them all here. But their lives go on and they needed to get home to their families. My sister Lorrie and her husband Sam came for a visit. Carol's sister Barb is still here but her daughter Ann left to go back to her own family. We have had over 5000 visits to our Caring Bridge page and hundreds of comments. I have had countless phone calls, texts, messages, emails and Facebook posts wishing us well. We've had a special friend send us gift cards for food, money deposited directly into our checking account and prayers by more people than I can even imagine. The outpouring of support for Carol and our family has been amazing and I thank you all. I know I can't send a thank you card to all of you or even send an electronic thank you, but we really do appreciate all the support.

As far as Carol's condition goes, there is not much to report. She continues to breathe on her own but is still unresponsive to stimuli. They are going to do another CT scan probably tomorrow. I'm not sure what they will be looking for but I guess they need to do it. I have lots of questions for the staff here at Grand Strand Medical Center but unfortunately they don't have a lot of answers. I guess it's the nature of severe brain trauma. Be patient and let God work it out.

For those of you concerned about my wellbeing, physically I am fine. I have been battling a sore throat and then a persistent cough for three weeks now but it is getting better. I had two lay doctors buy me some foul-tasting cough syrup yesterday and it actually is helping. Emotionally it's a roller coaster. Overall though I am doing fine. The situation is totally out my hands and there is nothing I can do to help other than pray a lot and be here for Carol. I'm working out regularly, eating a decent diet and taking time for myself. That's about all for now.

Day 16 Friday Night Journal entry by Bill Funnemark — 11/4/2016

I just needed some alone time this evening. Today's stay at the hospital was depressing. So when Barb and I got back to the condo I went for a short walk to a place Carol and I love, down to the beach. See Figure 7. I wish you could join me Carol.

Figure 7 The beach

Bill

Day 17 Saturday Afternoon Journal entry by Bill Funnemark — 11/5/2016

Wow! Is this really the 4th Saturday we've spent in Myrtle Beach? Yes it is. I left home on my motorcycle sometime October 7th. Carol was working in the Des Moines area that day and so we met at Mickolyn's house late that afternoon to ride along with Trent and Mickolyn to Will's football game. It would be the last one we would be able to attend but hoped we'd be able to watch the last two games of the season on The Cube, an Internet broadcast service, but they were not going to be broadcast. I left Mickolyn's home on Sunday or Monday, don't remember for sure, heading more or less for Myrtle Beach some 1200 miles away. Like a lot of my bike trips this one turned out to be a little longer than planned. So more like 2200 miles later I arrived in Myrtle Beach. Carol worked a few days and then on Wednesday night she flew to Ft. Worth to spend a couple days with the Hamells for Connor's birthday. Carol always tries to go see the grandkids on or near their birthdays. From there she flew to Myrtle Beach. So on Saturday the 15th, Carol, Ed, Becky and I all converged at Ocean 22 Hilton Grand Vacations for a fun filled week or so of fun. And it was fun until Thursday the 20th when Carol had her stroke.

So here we are still in South Carolina and life will never be the same. Even with the very best outcome, it will not be the same. Carol's chief neurosurgeon stopped in this morning and I was able to talk to him a little. She had another CT scan early this morning and he said it showed no additional bleeding but that there is still a lot of blood in the ventricles of her brain. There shouldn't be any there. He cannot give any long-term prognosis at this time. He did tell me that she would most likely be here for at least another couple weeks. Carol still is not responding to any stimuli but her vital signs are all in the normal range. She continues to have a drain from her brain in place to slowly remove the blood. Some of you have asked or wondered if they could do an EEG to measure brain function and the doctor said that it would serve no purpose. They already know she has brain function because she is breathing on her own as well as carrying on other normal body functions. Trust me. This is not some little Podunk backwater hospital. It is a regional trauma center and has some of the best doctors in the country. They know what they are doing and we have total confidence in their treatment. Carol is receiving excellent care. Even Carol would approve and that's saying a lot.

So for now I am planning to be here for a couple more weeks at least. Carol and I had purchased ownership in Hilton Grand Vacation Club a few years ago and through various circumstances we had accumulated a lot of points. Since I doubt Carol and I will be able to use these points anytime soon, we are using them to pay for our condo here in Myrtle Beach. We have already paid for them and if we don't use them we will lose them. This is not how either one of us had planned to use our points but in this case it has allowed me and my family to stay at a nice and convenient place with no cash outlay. I will be staying at Oceans 22 at least through November 23rd. If plans change I will certainly update this site.

Oceans 22 Hilton Grand Vacations
2200 N Ocean Blvd
Myrtle Beach, SC 29577

Again please do not send any flowers or a bunch of gifts since we really don't have a place for them. Carol's nephew continues to check our house and pick mail etc. but he is not forwarding mail to me here. So if anyone has sent cards or gifts to our home in Algona, I won't know about it for some time. But thank you all the same. I think that's all I have for today.

Bill

Day 17 Saturday Night Journal entry by Bill Funnemark — 11/5/2016

Just a short note for tonight. Nothing new to report on Carol. I just wanted to thank Barb, Carol's sister, and her daughter Ann for coming to be with me for a few days. Ann left Thursday afternoon and Barb is leaving in the morning. Tonight before we went back to our condo I took Barb to the little restaurant where Carol's ordeal began. We didn't eat there because she wanted to get back to our room so she could watch her beloved Iowa Hawkeyes. But the way the game is going I think we should have stayed to eat and forget about the game.

Figure 8 is Barb on the boardwalk.

Figure 8

Bill

Day 18 Sunday afternoon Journal entry by Bill Funnemark — 11/6/2016

Another week begins in Myrtle Beach. It is another beautiful day here but it sounds like it is warmer back in Algona. This morning it was 43 degrees at sunrise but it's warming up nicely. Carol's sister Barb headed back home this morning. It was so nice of her and her daughter Ann to drive Carol's Jeep out to me so I don't have to rent a car. These two ladies sort of spoiled me during their visit. They went grocery shopping for me cooked me some wonderful meals and were great company to have around. It was really tough for Barb to say goodbye this morning but it was just time for her to go home. Thanks Barb and Ann for coming to be with Carol and me.

So Barb went home but Steph's husband Pete arrived about the same time Barb was leaving. He plans on being here until Thursday. He asked Steph before he left if he'd have time to do some computer work. Steph assured him that yes you will have plenty of time to work on your computer. Most our day is spent sitting in Carol's room at the hospital. I will talk to her, rub her hand or her cheek but I get no answer. We've heard from plenty of folks who tell us to keep talking because Carol can hear you and sense your presence. I have no data to refute this, so we continue to let her know we are here. It sure would make it easier though if she would give me some kind of response. Maybe it's payback for all the times she would talk to me about things she'd done that day and maybe I wasn't listening that closely but at least I would nod or grunt once in a while. I'm sure there were many times when she knew I was listening more to a football game than I was about proper peri-care or some other procedure. I promise I will do a better job listening to you Carol if you wake up and start talking to me.

Not much is happening today. I'm sure some of you would like to hear more about what's going on with Carol, but the reality is, nothing much is happening. She is in a coma and just lies there. We just wait for her time to wake up or begin responding. I get the idea from the staff here not to expect much until more of the blood drains from her brain. We are all hoping that once this happens she will begin to show a more activity. God's timetable is not ours. So we wait.

That's about it for now.

Bill

**Day 19 Monday Morning Journal entry by Bill Funnemark —
11/7/2016**

After a week of virtually no news, I have something really positive to report this morning. No Carol didn't wake up or start responding to stimuli overnight, so that part hasn't changed. But she might be having a surgery later this week to replace the external brain drain tube with an internal one. Once that's in place and if she progresses like the doctors want, she can be transferred to Iowa. The timing on this depends on how her body responds and the availability of the appropriate facility for her continued treatment. As nice as Myrtle Beach is, I think we're all ready to be closer to home. This is just one of those many little steps on incredibly long journey. So I think she is still somewhere in the first few miles of her marathon. But at this point I praise God for any little positive step.

I know my journal entries have been getting shorter and for those of you who like to read my long rambling entries I'm sorry for the brevity. But the fact is there just isn't much to report. I can only comment on the beauty of the beach and the ocean so many times. I am doing fine physically. I have been fighting a cold and cough for several weeks but I think that has pretty well run its course. I have been eating well, working out fairly regularly and sleeping well at night, well most of the time. I do sometimes wake up early in the morning, way too early to get up, and look out at the ocean and just wonder what in the world has happened these last few weeks. What will our future bring? Will Carol and I ever go on vacations to the beach again? Will we be able to go see grandkids in Oregon or Texas or wherever they might be? So many questions, but I try not to dwell on them because I don't have the answers and worrying won't help anyone. So I just go day by day and trust that God has a plan for us and someday this plan will revealed to us all.

That's about all for now. Unless she does something really spectacular today or tomorrow, when she does wake up, the election will be over and hopefully she will be pleased with the winner. We both already voted but I won't tell you who she voted for because some of you would be pleased and some of you wouldn't. At this moment it doesn't matter to her and it's none of your business. LOL

Bill

Day 20 Tuesday Morning Journal entry by Bill Funnemark — 11/8/2016

Today is election day and I trust everyone will go vote. Since Carol and I knew we would be out of town part of October and that she might be busy at one of the many nursing homes where consults on this day, we both voted before we left for Myrtle Beach. I had planned to come home through Texas since this time of year is a great time to ride a motorcycle in the South and who knows how long it might take to get home. Little did we know that we'd still be in Myrtle Beach.

I usually write my journal entry while sitting in Carol's hospital room but not this morning. Pete and I haven't made it there yet. I planned to go for a run this morning and as I lie in bed looking out at the sunrise over the Atlantic Ocean, I just kept procrastinating and then I checked the temperature, 43 degrees, and decided an afternoon run would be a better idea. So I decided I would watch one of the DVDs of recent church services a friend sent. I hadn't even taken the time to open the box yet. To my surprise, besides the DVDs, there is also an Applebee's gift card. Thank you my friend. Then I thought I should check my bank account to see if there was any money in my checking account. I actually knew there was, but a friend had told me they'd made a gift deposit and I just wanted to make sure it was there. To my amazement there were two other deposits I knew nothing about. One of them I recognized the name and have already thanked them this morning. The other I have no idea who she is. Whoever you, are Carol and I thank you.

Last night when Pete and I left the hospital I was really discouraged and confused. There are just so many things to think about and worry about if I let myself. I try not to dwell on the things I can't control, like how much will all this cost. We have Medicare and insurance which will cover the bulk of the costs, but I know there will be some expense for us. I can't even imagine how much the hospital bill is at this point. 18 days in NSICU isn't cheap. But I'm not worried about this. I'm more concerned about how Carol's recovery will progress, how we'll get her to Iowa, where will she be placed, how will I get my baby (Triumph Trophy motorcycle) home and just a myriad of concerns. But this morning after watching the church service from a couple weeks ago and with the blessing I had this morning, I just feel so much better. Thank you everyone for your continued prayers and support.

Bill

Day 21 Wednesday Afternoon Journal entry by Bill Funnemark — 11/9/2016

Pete and I both stayed up way too late last night watching election results. I wasn't planning on watching it but I got sucked into it like many of you did. So I'm running a little slowly today. Of course I always run a little slowly. Today Carol is supposed to have surgery to place a shunt in her head to drain the fluid in her brain that currently is being handled by an external drain. We are looking forward to moving Carol to a Long Term Acute Care, LTAC, facility. Once her external drain is replaced she can be transferred to a facility that specializes in patients like Carol. We don't know for sure where or when she will be moved but my best guess is that we will be moving to a LTAC near Charleston, SC sometime early next week. Although we'd all love to have her back in Iowa, her doctor doesn't think she would tolerate a 20+ hour ambulance trip. It's estimated she will be in the LTAC about three weeks. Depending how she progresses, it is hoped we can come back to Iowa after that time.

At this time I have no idea what kinds of disabilities Carol might have when she wakes up. It is impossible to tell right now how much damage has occurred and where this damage is located. We know she has some function because she is breathing on her own, she is processing food, her heart is beating strongly, kidneys are working and so on. We know her muscles work at least to some extend because she will move reflexively. We won't know the extent of her brain damage until she wakes up and starts to communicate with us. The LTAC is designed for rehabilitation, to begin the process of getting Carol back to being a fully functional woman. One who can smile at her grandchildren, go to their ballgames, concerts, homecoming parades, graduations and weddings. A woman who can enjoy the ocean with me and our friends again. A wife who has always been my biggest supporter. A woman who left her family and followed me to far away Georgia a few days after we were married to Robins AFB where she knew no one. She made the best of it and learned to love the deep south. Carol has always been a strong woman but so full of love. I know that Carol will want to get back to work in her retirement too. Those of you who don't know her quite so well, Carol worked at Good Samaritan Care Center for 30 years and was Director of Nursing Services for 25 of those years. When she retired on a Friday, now almost three years ago, she took the weekend off and then on Monday began a career as a nurse consultant. People ask me what she does in this job and I really don't know. What I do know is that she absolutely loves it and the facilities where she consults love and respect her as well. So I know she will want to get back to work.

We all just want her to wake up. So day by day we go looking for any little step in the right direction. Keep praying for her. Remember this is a marathon, not a sprint and we're just barely getting started.

Bill

Day 21 Transportation Journal entry by Chad Funnemark — 11/9/2016

I know so many of you have already helped out, and that is amazing. The prayers, kind words, emotional support have been more than we could have imagined.

My dad spoke with the air ambulance people, and they recommended we try a GoFundMe site. So, we have. We also posted it on Facebook, so hopefully it will be seen. Although our dad can stay wherever our mom is, we think it would be so much easier on everyone if they could be back in Iowa.

Day 22 Afternoon Journal entry by Bill Funnemark — 11/10/2016

Somehow I got off on my day count. We've actually begun Day 22. This all began around 1:15 PM on October 20th. Not much has happened with Carol today. She was supposed to have surgery yesterday afternoon to put in a shunt, but that got postponed until late this morning and then to around 5:00 PM today. So I'm still waiting. Her condition has not changed. This morning Pete and I came to the hospital early so he could spend a little time with Carol before his flight back to Texas. I took him to the airport and he was to leave Myrtle Beach around 9:30 this morning. I ran a couple quick errands and came back to the hospital so I could be here before they took Carol to surgery, only to learn it had been postponed.

A case worker from the hospital came and talked to me and answered a lot of questions about what to expect in the next few days and then in the next few weeks. Some of it good news and some not so good. We were hoping to be able to bring Carol back to a LTAC, Long Term Acute Care, facility in Des Moines, but there are none that are appropriate for her needs. So our best option is Regency Hospital Company in Florence, SC. It is about an hour from Myrtle Beach and is a top notch facility. It is also close enough to MB that I can stay in my current condo without having worry about moving. We still have a few Hilton points, so if I need to stay a little longer I still have that option. But so far I have spent very little on lodging since we have already paid for the points we are using. This just isn't how we envisioned using our vacation points when we bought them. But what a godsend that we have them.

Since I will be staying in Myrtle Beach and commuting back and forth between here and Florence in the near future, I plan to keep my motorcycle here in MB and ride it back and forth. I figure if I can commute to school and back each day in northern Iowa usually into December, I should be able to handle it in South Carolina. But at some point I do need to get it back in Iowa. One of my dear CWL families is working on that though. I even had a friend of Stephanie from Texas, a Harley rider to boot, offer to somehow ride it back. We'll get it figured out.

We had hoped to be able to come back to Iowa in a few days and were looking into an air ambulance service. But that is really expensive and since there is no appropriate place for Carol, that's on hold. At some point we will still need to transport her back to Iowa when the time is right. I was hesitant asking for gifts from anyone, although many of you have already sent me things. gift cards or cash and each little gift is so appreciated. But I just couldn't start asking for money to help with an air ambulance or many other expenses we will incur. Our wonderful son Chad, who by the way, will retire from the Air Force in May

2017* (Happy Veterans Day Chad), took it upon himself to set up a Go Fund Me page. He did get my permission before it went live. We have been absolutely blown away by the generosity of all of you. One of the wonders of social media is that it reaches so many people in such a short time. Friends contact friends, who contact more friends. It is the classic pyramid scheme that actually works. I know we can't thank all of you personally but speaking for my whole family, a huge thank you.

They are just coming now to take Carol to surgery. So say a prayer that all goes well.

That's all for now.

Bill

*Chad delayed his retirement until March 3, 2018.

Day 22 Mom, you need to wake up because we need you and you're missing stuff

Journal entry by Mickolyn Clapper — 11/10/2016

I haven't done any of these posts because I'm generally pretty private, but so many people are following this so I feel like it's my turn to contribute. And for once I'd like to write something that's not part of my dissertation and doesn't have to be supported with evidence. So here goes

Do you ever just have a moment when it just hits you? I was driving home from work and I was thinking that Mom is supposed to be here. She told me she'd stay with the kids when Trent and I went to Vegas. We're at the airport right now and she's not at my house spoiling the boys and Della (our dog who she spoils). She missed Will's 16th birthday.

She missed his last football game as a Raider and the pride of hearing he made first team all-district. You know that would have made Facebook with all of us tagged. Anyway, I was driving home from school today and then the song "Praise You in the Storm" by Casting Crowns came on and I really listened to it. I mean I really listened to the words and I just cried. I cried because this is so hard and because there's nothing I can do to fix any of it. It was the same song that was on the radio the day mom called me to say don't freak out but Dad is in the ER. He might be having a heart attack.* The words are powerful and sad and this just really sucks. So after I bawled all the way from Nevada to Collins, I turned to Jimmy Buffett and listened to Boat Drinks instead. Mom hates riding with me because she does not share my fondness for the XM station Margaritaville. Anyway thanks to Lena for stepping in to help with the kids. They are blessed with two wonderful grandmas.

Mickolyn

*I did not have a heart attack

Day 22 Quick Update Journal entry by Stephanie Hamell — 11/10/2016

I know dad will give a full report in the morning, but I know some people were waiting to hear how the surgery went. Dad said the doc reported that it went well, she's resting back in her room. Pete is back in Texas so Dad is holding down the fort in South Carolina until some of us make our next trip out there. Thanks again for all of the prayers. Of course we all have moments when we are a mess, but truly the prayers help us get through these long days when we have more questions than answers. Thanks again for all of the support. It really means the world to us.

Steph

Day 23 Journal entry by Bill Funnemark — 11/11/2016

Just a quick note to Carol's many friends and followers. Carol had a good night after a successful surgery to put in the shunt. There is no change in her condition. Sorry for the short post, but I'm not having a very good day.

Thank you all for your prayers. We all really need them, Carol most of all.

Bill

Day 24 Journal entry by Bill Funnemark — 11/12/2016

Sorry for the late update all of you, but I'm finally getting a chance to sit down and compose some thoughts. This afternoon around 3:00 Carol was moved from NSICU to what's called a step-down unit. She is still in Grand Strand Medical Center, just not in the ICU. Once the doctor removed her external drain and replaced it with the internal shunt, she was no longer a candidate for the ICU. There has been no change in her condition for the last nearly three weeks. She is still getting the same kind of care as she was in the ICU but she just has fewer machines connected to her.

I spent some time with her this morning while she was still in the ICU and then took a Triumph ride to Whiteville, NC, about an hour away, to visit my sister Lorrie and her husband Sam. I'd never been there before so it was a good time to go for a visit and a good day for a ride. Sam gave me a brief tour of the town and then Lorrie fed me some lunch. So those of you who are concerned about my dietary needs, let me assure you that I'm not going hungry. Of course some of my diet consists of goodies from The Chocolate Season or Reese's and circus peanuts, compliments of Chad Funnemark. But I also have received a few gift cards from friends to restaurants with real food. And I have food in my refrigerator.

My days do tend to drag a little but I'm doing ok. I've had visitors up until this weekend. So I will have a few days on my own, but next week my pastor is coming for a visit. The following week some family will be here for Thanksgiving. Really, is Thanksgiving that close? I'm doing ok.

Bill

Day 25 Journal entry by Bill Funnemark — 11/13/2016

This morning is cool and a little rainy. Cool for me but probably cold for Myrtle Beach. The forecast is for rain off and on today and since I need to go to the grocery store later, I decided to drive the Jeep. Tomorrow our pastor is flying in and will be here for a couple days. It will be good to see another familiar face. Plus he's bringing me a few more clothes. When I left home I brought one pair of jeans and a couple pairs of shorts. It appears that shorts weather might be about over.

Carol is resting comfortably this morning and there doesn't appear to be any change in her condition. Sometime after I left last night, they removed the bandage covering her shunt incision. That appears to be healing nicely although at the moment it looks a little scary. But after a couple more days they will be able to clean it better. I think Carol is still on schedule to be transferred to the LTAC facility sometime this week depending on bed availability in that facility.

One of my very dear friends sent me this T-shirt. It says:

"Strong to the Finish, Finish the Race. Keep the Faith."

2 Timothy 4:7 "I have fought the good fight, I have finished the race, I have kept the faith." Thanks Kerianne.

Thanks for all your prayers and support in so many ways.

Bill

Day 25 Just a message of thanks Journal entry by Stephanie Hamell — 11/13/2016

I don't really have an update, I am just finally taking time to thank everyone who has supported our family in some way. It may have been a gift card, a homemade meal, a card, a gift of money, muffins, rides for our boys, rides home from the airport, people reaching out to help in some special way through email or Facebook, and all of the prayers and well-wishes. This experience has just confirmed how special my mom is, and how good people are in general.

I hate that I can't be in South Carolina to support my dad and to watch over my mom. I know she is in good hands and that does give me peace. The longer she is in a coma the more desperate I become to hear her voice, or receive a text from her telling me to wish the boys luck, or that she's praying for Pete's job search or any number of things. I want to see her Facebook posts where she tags everyone who is in anyway involved in the post. I ache to call her when I'm driving somewhere. I could be consumed with this, I could give into despair, but I can't, I won't. My mom loves her family fiercely and no matter what she never gives up on any of us. She is a prayer warrior like no one I know. I know she has a long a road ahead, I will continue to pray for a miracle every day. Our faith has sustained us through this time, God has given me peace that I can't understand. It is has been a true blessing to see God working in our lives and others.

For now I will settle for reading old texts from her, looking at her Facebook page and when I can't bear not hearing her voice anymore I call her cell phone to listen to outgoing voicemail message. I will continue to give thanks and glory and praise to God. He has blessed us in so many ways, most of all He gives us the opportunity to have hope. For without him, we would have none. So thank you all.

Day 26 Journal entry by Bill Funnemark — 11/14/2016

Yesterday in Myrtle Beach was overcast and rainy. This morning it's just overcast with temperatures in the low 50's. Because of the clouds I didn't get a chance to see the special full moon last night. I'll just have to wait until the next time. Carol has been in the PCU or stepdown unit for almost 2 days now. Carol is still getting good care but there is a definite difference between the NSICU and the PCU. In the NSICU a nurse came in at least hourly and they always had time to spare to listen to our concerns, get to know us and let us get to know them. They would freely offer a hug whenever they sensed a need. They are very special people there. The PCU is just different. Christina, a very nice young woman, is very efficient and I think very competent but I don't see her nearly as often. Not because she doesn't care but she has many more patients to cover. It's just the nature of not being in an ICU.

Carol has not changed. There is still no response to stimuli. She continues to breathe on her own with just the benefit of a trach collar. A trach collar is just a little plastic shell-like device that sits loosely over her trach opening. Humidified, oxygenated air just blows by the hole. It is up to Carol to draw it in on her own. All her vitals remain strong and right in the range where they should be,

Each day I send out an email update to some of our family and to some close friends. I give a little more personal information that I don't care to share with the entire world. In my update today I mentioned how it's ironic that although this is a crisis to me and 26 days ago it was to all of you, but as time goes on Carol gets moved from front page, above the fold news to below the fold and then off the front page entirely. I understand this completely and I don't blame any of you. After all if you are still reading my daily updates you are still concerned. We all appreciate your prayers and kind words and kind actions and support. I read every response and I check to see who is still visiting this site. But just like each of you, I too am getting tired of this whole new world. I'm not giving up or anything like that, but it is a real drag. We all just want Carol back and to show some response so that I know she's still with us. It is hard to sit here each day and think about what we should be doing back in Iowa or what we're missing.

There have been so many acts of kindness from so many people that my family and I are just amazed. Our children live in Iowa, Texas and Oregon but our support team covers the country. One of the benefits of social media is to share news in an incredibly fast and far reaching manner. I get up each day and usually after a workout and breakfast, I head to the hospital. Sitting here by Carol's side for hours at a time makes for a long day. And then I go back to my new home and go to bed to get ready for another day of the same. Don't get me wrong, I wouldn't be anywhere else but it does get to be a drag. Your positive and uplifting comments either in Caring Bridge or through a personal message is what helps keep me going. Thank you for sticking with us and thank you for your prayers and support.

Our pastor arrived in Myrtle Beach today.

Bill

Day 26 Looking Good! Go for it! Journal entry by Chad Funnemark — 11/14/2016

Everyday my dad writes an update about my mom. I really appreciate these and the comments that everyone posts. It is so amazing to see the words people share and to see how much love there is out there for my mom. Today, I wanted to share a little different post. I thought I'd share a funny memory.

I'm not sure what year it was; I'm guessing maybe 1985'ish. For some unknown reason to me, my dad decided he was going to run Grandma's Marathon. I didn't know what that was at the time. I'd seen my dad run countless 5K and 10K races around the Algona area. It seemed like every little town had a fun run with their summer festival. But, I had no idea what a marathon was. We used to camp a lot as a family then, and there happened to be a "rustic" campground around mile 13 called Scenic 61. It made for a very convenient location to watch the runners go by about midway through the race.

The family loaded up before the crack of dawn and drove 13 miles north to Two Harbors, MN. There were all sorts of traffic and people, but we made it. My dad got down to the starting line and the race began. Now, my mom had to maneuver through all these people and cars to get to the halfway point before we missed him. Most people were letting a car in, then another car afterwards… the zipper effect. She was already super stressed about not making it back to the campground in time. A funny thing (at least to me,) happened… someone in a Bronco cut my mom off. She said something to effect of, "I'd like to flip him off, but that's not nice. Instead, I'll give him the Christian Fist!" And, she sure did! I doubt he saw it, or cared if he did. It really surprised us.

The other part of the story was one of the volunteers who was working by the campground said, "Looking good! Go for it!" about once every 5 seconds, and then repeated it. We were next to her for maybe an hour.... We saw our dad run past, and then we rushed in Duluth to see him finish. He did, and we were all happy, and I'm sure there was more stress on my mom getting into Duluth and finding the finish.

Maybe because of the marathon references my dad is using to describe this journey, or maybe another reason, but this story popped into my head. So, Mom, go ahead and give whoever you need to the Christian Fist and wake up!! We want you back! "Looking Good! Go for it!!

Love you Mom!
Chad

Day 27 Journal entry by Bill Funnemark — 11/15/2016

I awoke this morning to the sound of the ocean waves crashing far below my bedroom window. These aren't waves of surfing championships size but they will do. I look out and I can't really see the Atlantic because, one it's 4:00 AM and two it's foggy as can be. So I lie there for a bit, decide I might as well get up and go to the bathroom and go back to bed. Seemed like a good time to go back to sleep. Guess again. I start thinking about some of Carol's favorite songs, most of which are old hymns but also some newer songs by Christian singers. And then out the blue I think of this one song that our dear friend AJ would sing in church usually around Christmas time. I'm trying to go back to sleep but I can't get the song out of my mind. I can't remember enough of it to even do a Google search for it. So AJ if you read this, I'm sure you will remember the song and please email or text me with the name of it, because it's driving me batty and Carol probably isn't going to tell me this morning either.

So after giving up on going back to sleep, I decide rather reluctantly to go ahead and get dressed for my morning workout. It's still dark out and really too foggy to safely run outside, so off I go to the fitness center, being careful not to wake Peter as I leave. (I just heard his alarm as I'm writing this but no other sounds from his room. So I guess he's not quite ready to face the day yet.) I do my workout, come back to my room and sit down for a cup of coffee. Our son-in-law Pete Hamell, not to be confused with Pastor Peter, was here last week for a few days. He needed to go to a bookstore one day and while he couldn't find the book he wanted, he did buy a devotional book for me. He suggested that yes even though I've been writing a journal online for all of you, I should maybe start writing a private one for myself in the space alongside each day's devotion. My intentions were good Pete, but I have to admit that I haven't started yet. This morning I read the devotion and it just seemed so appropriate. There were various passages of scripture that reminded me to keep my body fit and to stay physically strong. As Chad mentioned in his post yesterday, I run marathons. I made a decision many years ago to lose some weight and do a better job of staying fit. Actually it was Dr. Moss from the Kossuth Regional Health Center who threatened me back in 1983 with "lose weight or else" type conversation that really got me going. Since then I have tried to stay somewhat fit. I wanted to be around to get old with Carol and to see my children and grandchildren do the things we love to watch.

These last few days I can't help but wonder if Carol is going to be with me on this journey. Carol is running her own marathon right now. Anyone who has ever run a marathon or done something similar knows there comes a time in every race when you "Hit the Wall". It doesn't seem to matter if you are fast or slow you still hit the wall. I usually hit the wall around mile 17 or 18 but it varies. While running my first marathon in Duluth, MN I hit the wall at a spot around mile 22 called Lemon Drop Hill and then a few blocks later on another hill. I was running, or maybe barely moving, up this hill feeling I wasn't going to make it and maybe I'd just quit. My family would eventually find me lying in a heap along the curb. When I was at my lowest point physically and mentally, a complete stranger came along side of me and started talking to me all the way up the hill and then he disappeared. I never saw him again. I'm not saying he was an angel, although he could have been, but more likely God put him there at that moment to encourage me so I could make it up that last big hurdle.

I don't know what God has in store for Carol and me and my family, but I know God is with us all. I think today we are all at our own Lemon Drop Hill. It may not be mile 22 but it is still a struggle. I am doing what I can for Carol but I can't do much on my own. Carol really needs her own angel to help her on her journey. We still don't know what mile we're on or where the next turn will take us but we do know that God is in control. So each day we do what we can and pray for some good news to come our way.

And Pastor Peter did finally get up.

Bill

Day 28 Journal entry by Bill Funnemark — 11/16/2016

Wow. Has it really been this long. In about 30 minutes from now we will begin the 28th day of our journey and before I'm done writing, the time will have passed into that next day. First off like yesterday and the day before and the day before that and so on, there is no change in Carol. She is still in a coma and still unresponsive. This morning when Pastor Peter and I walked into her room, she just looked so peaceful. It's like she is just taking a nap and having a pleasant dream. Probably remembering riding around in our little Audi TT convertible, top down, wind in her hair on our way to some quaint little restaurant for a meal. And of course she'd take a picture of my food.

This whole experience has been and continues to be like a bad dream. I think each morning I will awake and Carol will be beside me in our bed sharing the view of the ocean. But then I turn over and she's not there. But this experience has been so humbling and gratifying to read all the comments of support. To see the generosity in your gifts. Our Go Fund Me account has grown larger than any of us every expected. We've had organizations tell me that they are foregoing their Christmas parties and sending the money they would have spent to help get Carol back to Iowa. I don't know what our next step will be. It seems that we make a plan and then something changes and we make a new plan. Carol's lack of progress has caused us to reevaluate everything as far as the kind of care that is most appropriate. If that care is best given here in South Carolina, we'll stay here a while longer. If the care she needs is best given in Iowa, we'll come home. This is a decision our family along with Carol's medical staff will have to decide. But for now we're staying in Myrtle Beach at least through next week. Of course this could always change too.

I started this about two hours ago and I think I'm done for today. Too many interruptions.

Bill

Day 29 Journal entry by Bill Funnemark — 11/17/2016

By the time I finish today's entry, we will be beginning the 29th day of this marathon, October 20, 2016 about 1:15 PM eastern time. I just arrived at the hospital a few minutes ago after taking Pastor Peter to the airport for his flight back home. It has been a comfort to have had him here for a visit. He came under very difficult circumstances but we made the best of it. Even though he has been our pastor for some time now, I didn't really know him and he really didn't know Carol or me.

Our time together here gave us both a chance to learn about each other and for him to learn who Carol is through me. Thank you to the Elders of our church for sending him here.

We have had a few very cool days here of late but today is just absolutely beautiful, clear and probably around 70. Even Carol's hospital room is comfortable today. Some days for whatever reason they keep it really cold in her room, but not today. I'm not complaining. Carol is lying comfortably, no motion, no response to any voice commands or any other stimuli, just lying there like she is sound asleep. I have not seen a doctor, nurse or case worker yet since I just got here, but I'm sure someone will be stopping by soon. As far as I can tell there have been no changes since yesterday or for the last 25 days.

Last night after Peter and I left the hospital, we went to Moo Moon's on the boardwalk for a sandwich before heading back to the condo. We sat at the same table where Ed, Becky, Carol and I sat 28 days ago. I had the Hangover Burger like I did that day. I'm not sure if it's supposed to cure or create a hangover. It did neither for me. It is just a really good, probably not so healthy, sandwich. I warned Peter to stay away from the Shrimp Po Boy, the sandwich Carol ate. We were able to laugh a little but also were saddened by the memories. The manager who was on duty that day was there too, and I spoke to her briefly but had no good news for her. Peter walked back to the condo along the beach and tried to find a t-shirt store so he could buy a few gifts to take home. Luckily there are only a few hundred such shops. I went back, picked up some mail, bought a salted caramel mocha and went down by the beach to just be alone with my thoughts. Oh how Carol loves the ocean. We would spend hours just sitting in a beach chair, reading or snoozing or talking or just watching and listening to the waves. The empty chair beside me still feels so unnatural.

When I went back upstairs I opened my mail, a care package from Z, a former CWL student now living in Hermantown, MN. Z isn't her real name, but that's what I called her because there were two girls named Emily in my class and Z was just easier. She will always be Z to me. I also got a gift card to some bakery that I will need to explore tomorrow. It sounds yummy, but how can you go wrong in a bakery. Thanks Sara.

One other item. The Chocolate Season of Algona, Iowa fame, is helping raise funds to bring Carol back to Iowa. Erika, the owner of the store, is donating a portion of her income to our Go Fund Me account. I don't like to self-promote a fundraiser, but I do want to thank Erika for her efforts. We go way back to when she was just a baby. I held her almost every Sunday in church and she spent the time playing with my beard. We've both grown past that stage but she remains a dear friend. Thanks Brad and Erika.

That's about all for today.

Bill

Day 30 Journal entry by Bill Funnemark — 11/18/2016

Thirty days has September, April, June and November. All the rest have thirty-one, except February which has twenty-eight, except on leap year. Maybe they don't teach this little mnemonic in school anymore, but it's one that has been with me since I was a little kid. Yes, we will soon be entering the thirtieth day of our journey. A whole month has past. Hundreds or maybe thousands of people have been praying for God to do a miracle and heal my beloved Carol for this past month. And God may still do this. I don't know. My children don't know. Our pastor doesn't know. Her doctors don't know. No one knows if God is going to heal Carol and bring her back to who she was at 1:00 PM on

October 20, 2016 or will God allow her to remain who she became at 1:15 PM on October 20, 2016. We just don't know.

I had a long video chat with Stephanie, Mickolyn and Chad last night and we agreed that we don't know either. We have not given up hope. But we also came to the realization that God has already worked a miracle. This isn't the miracle we have been praying for and I'm not saying God won't perform another miracle and restore Carol. We just don't know. We do know that many, many people have been drawn much closer to God as a result of our family crisis. I don't know if someone has been lead to accept Jesus as the Lord and Savior, but I believe that there is at least one person who has been moved to a more meaningful relationship with God. Carol prayed about everything and all the time. Every time I would head off on a motorcycle trip, she would pray for me and that I would have safe travels. She prayed for her children and grandchildren every day.

I stayed up quite late last night after our video chat writing some long overdue emails and just tending to some business. I had planned to sleep in. I am here by myself, so I have no one to entertain or answer to and there is no rush to get to the hospital. So I planned to catch up for lost sleep. But no. At about 6:00 as it is just starting to get light, I find myself fully awake. So I made some coffee, put on some sweats and went down to the beach to watch the sunrise and spend a little time with God. I decided to pass on my morning workout today and just spend some quiet time. Like I said above, I don't know what is going to happen to Carol in the next few days, few weeks or longer. But this morning walking and sitting on the beach with my coffee I felt an incredible peace that I haven't had in weeks. God is telling me something. I haven't quite figured it out yet, but I'm at peace with whatever happens. God has already worked a miracle through Carol in a way I or my children would have never imagined or planned. God will take care of Carol, of my three children and my nine grandchildren. It is a great day to be alive. God is good.

Figure 9 Sunrise on Myrtle Beach, SC 11/18/2016. What a beautiful morning.

Figure 9

Bill

Day 31 Journal entry by Bill Funnemark — 11/19/2016

No change in Carol's condition today. Today was a beautiful day in Myrtle Beach, probably better than in the Midwest. This morning seemed like a good day for a ride. So I rode to Whiteville, NC to where my sister Lorrie lives. I left my bike there and she gave me a ride back. Some friends from Corwith are driving out in December to load it on a trailer and take it back to Iowa. I figure I will be heading back to Iowa myself pretty soon, so that is just one more detail checked off my list of things to do. Tomorrow is supposed to be just as nice too. I think a run on the beach is in order. A couple days ago a dear friend gave me a gift card to a local breakfast eatery. I had mentioned this to one of the young ladies who helps with Carol and she said I had to try Chicken Waffles. I thought it a strange combination, but she assured me it was delicious. So what the heck. It was a plate sized waffle with three large chicken strips on top of it. Either would have been enough for a meal by itself. Together it was almost too much. I found it a little strange but ok I guess, especially if you really like chicken, which I don't. But that's another story for another day.

When I got to the hospital today, I decided I should go back to the NSICU to give an update on Carol's status. I had no idea if any of her nurses would be on duty. But two of her nurses who spent a lot of time with Carol were there. Tanya, one of the nurses who was on duty from the moment Carol arrived on the afternoon of the 20th was there. She is a wonderful woman and an example of what a nurse is supposed to be. Carol and Tanya would have been friends had they had the chance. It was really nice to see both of these two women who spent so much time with Carol and our family. They helped us survive through the first terrible few hours and days.

I wish I had more to report but there just isn't a lot to say. I think things will be changing soon but I'm not ready to elaborate to the whole world just yet what may be happening soon. It seems that whenever a plan starts to take shape, the plan changes. So I will just not say anything until I know for sure. Carol is still in a coma and unresponsive, which is the way she has been for the last 27 days.

Keep praying. And remember God has already worked miracles through Carol's journey. So far it's not the miracle we've been asking for but miracles still have happened. Thanks for all your support.

Bill

As I mentioned a few pages back, each day when I wrote my Caring Bridge entry, I also wrote a family update email. This was sent to family and a few close friends. I never lied in my Caring Bridge posts, but I didn't always give all the information I had, or share some secrets that I held back. Talking to the medical staff lead me to believe very early on that Carol would not survive and would probably never regain consciousness. I continued to hold out hope to friends and family, but by Day 4, it was clear to me she was not getting better. Some of my conversations in the next few days confirmed what we all were afraid would be the reality of Carol's life.

This is my Family Update.
From: **Bill Funnemark**
Date: Sat, Nov 19, 2016 at 4:29 PM
Subject: Saturday Update

Good afternoon everyone. I've had a busy day and now am finally getting to my job of updating everyone. I'll get around to Caring Bridge later. It's a beautiful day in Myrtle Beach and so I decided it was time to ride my bike to my sister Lorrie's house in North Carolina, about an hour away. I'm leaving it there for now and in a couple weeks, friends from Corwith are driving out with a trailer and will haul it back home for me. Then Lorrie brought me back to Myrtle Beach.

The reason I needed to do this now is that Carol and I are coming home. Some of you already know some or all the details and others of you don't. It's getting a little confusing trying to remember who we've told and who we haven't so this is the latest update. On Thursday I talked to Carol's doctor to get his assessment of her. The short answer, and he was very thorough in his explanation but I'm not going give you everything he said, is that Carol is not going to get better. He can't say for sure, no one can. But in his professional view, since there has been essentially no response to stimuli for 24 days, he does not think there ever will be. The fact that she did respond to voice commands in the first three days gave us hope. Something happened to Carol's brain around day four. There was a noticeable change from some response to no response. Our kids saw the change and they know that there was hope and then it seemed to be gone. We still believed there was hope of improvement for many days to come, but with absolutely nothing happening, our hope started to fade. I think our kids still held on to some hope because they were not here day after day, but the longer I sit here the more discouraged I become.

Last Monday her doctor pretty much confirmed my feelings but wanted to give it a few more days. But when he looked at her this past Thursday, I think he came to the conclusion that she was not getting better. So, any talk of rehab centers quickly faded. I do not want to put Carol through those kinds of stresses whatever they might be for no apparent reason.

Thursday night Chad set up a video chat with Steph, Mickolyn, Chad and me. We talked for nearly three hours about that day's events and how we want to proceed. The four of us are in total agreement with what should and will happen next. And this in itself is a tremendous weight of my shoulders and I think for them too. We talked very openly, no holding back. We used words like death and dying and funeral and all those words no one wants to say out loud, but we have to. So this is what is going to happen.

Monday, November 21st at 6:00 AM Carol will be discharged from the hospital in Myrtle Beach. An ambulance is scheduled to pick her up at 7:00 AM to begin a nearly 24-hour ride back to Iowa. Once she arrives in Algona, she will be admitted into Good Samaritan Care Center. Yes, this is the same care center where she worked for 30 years and was Director of Nursing for 25 years. She will be going into a hospice unit. Carol is already on a DNR (Do Not Resuscitate) order. Once in Good Samaritan, Hospice of the Heartland will be working with Carol and our family to make Carol comfortable. I don't know how long she will last, but her doctor indicated that it would probably be a matter of a few weeks. At that point some secondary problem will come up and Carol's body will just not be able to fight it off.

Some of you already know this part of our story but I wanted everyone in this group to know where we are. As I told my kids in our video chat, I believe that the Carol who I knew and loved for nearly 50 years, died somewhere around October 24th. The part of her brain that made her Carol is gone and what is left just runs her breathing and heart and things like that. We may be wrong and will never know. God could perform a miracle and she might wake up. But that sure doesn't appear to be the case. I have accepted that fact that I will never have my Carol back in this life. Our three children agree with me. They may still hold a glimmer of hope the same as I do, but we are prepared to let Mom go because we are pretty sure she has already gone. She's already in Heaven.

As for me, I will load up all our stuff from our condo after seeing the ambulance off and drive back to Algona. We will have family at Good Sam to welcome Carol home and I will be there when I get there, probably Wednesday sometime. I am not sharing all of this on Caring Bridge. We don't want the whole world to know all of Carol's story just yet. But we also realize that we can't keep it a secret very long. Out of respect for Carol and our family, I do ask that you try not to spread any of this around. Let Carol come home first.

You are in this group because you are special to me in some way. Some of you are related and can't help it. Some of you are just special friends. But you are all very special to me and to Carol. God has already worked a miracle, it's just not the same miracle most of us were praying for.

Love you all,
Bill

Day 32 Journal entry by Bill Funnemark — 11/20/2016

It is 4:00 AM EST as I sit down to write and I've been awake for a couple hours now. My granddaughter Courtney has proof since we were texting back and forth an hour ago. She's a freshman at Drake University in Des Moines. So it was either pretty late for her or very early. I'm guessing it was getting late. So I finally got up, made some coffee and am listening to Christmas music. I woke a while ago and started thinking of things Carol will miss or has already missed. She was able to wish Chad a happy birthday via a text, phone call or post on Facebook before we left on vacation. On her way to Myrtle Beach she stopped in Texas to wish Connor a happy birthday a little bit early. Carol always made sure each of the grandkids got a birthday card and a gift, even if we couldn't always be there. Sometime during this ordeal I realized that we had missed Will Clapper's birthday. Grandma just didn't get a card and a gift sent. I assured Will that I will take care of it when I get back to Iowa. Carol is going to miss her brother-in-law Tim Long's birthday coming up in just a few days. She's going to miss Thanksgiving and a couple days after that is Mickolyn's birthday. Then a few weeks later is Stephanie's birthday. Then Christmas and then more grandkids' birthdays. Will Carol be with us for any of these or not?

Carol has always loved Christmas for so many reasons. First and foremost we celebrate the birth of Jesus Christ. But the whole season was such a joy for her. We (mostly Carol) would decorate the house inside and out. She would have me string lights all over the place. She always had to put garland on the front steps. Over the years the outside lights got fewer as my enthusiasm for crawling up and down ladders waned. But it would take weeks to decorate inside and even longer to put it all away. A few years ago she went to a much smaller tree that just stays up all year. But as she reduced the holiday decorations she would increase the present buying. It wasn't unusual for her to be buying this or that in July for one of the kids or grandkids but by Christmas she'd forgotten she'd bought it. Maybe she'd find it in March. It's hard telling what I might find stashed around the house. I remember not so many years ago we found a Far Side desk calendar that she'd got for me but forgot to wrap it. Luckily enough time had passed and the days of the week matched up with the numbers again, well at least until February 29th.

Carol loves Christmas music and so this morning I'm sitting here enjoying a cup of coffee listening to some of our favorite Christmas songs. We have similar tastes in music. We like traditional hymns but we also like contemporary songs. I especially like ones by the Staler Brothers, some are gospel type songs and others just good family type songs but all of them stress the real reason for Christmas. Carol's favorite Christmas song and maybe her overall favorite is a song recorded by Kenny Roger called "Christmas Everyday" which I mentioned several days go. Again one very early morning I woke thinking about that song but I could not remember the name or the artist. I just knew that our friend AJ sang it several times in church. AJ quickly responded that she knew exactly what song I was referring to and proceeded to type the full lyrics in a message to me. I played it the next day for Carol at the hospital.

What else will Carol miss? As I think about how the future will be different no matter Carol's outcome I wonder if she will ever get to ride in our little Audi? Will we be able to go to Florida for a few weeks this spring? We were going to go in January since that seems like a good time not to be in Iowa and southern Florida seemed a lot more appealing. But then we decided we would miss too many of Will's basketball games. And maybe we could sneak down to Texas to watch a few ball games down there too. Carol is going to miss them too and probably our late winter trip to the beach.

Today is Harvest Home at First Baptist (Grace) Church. I know many churches have a tradition like this that goes back many years. For us it has changed over the years as far as the actual service, but the constant is always a huge Thanksgiving meal. Although I really don't need all the food I will miss this occasion. There is always lots of turkey and pie and those are really the only two things that matter. What am I thankful for this year? Well I'm not thankful that Carol is in the hospital. But I am thankful for my family who are spread around the country. I am thankful for so many friends and strangers who have reached out to me these past 31 days. Some of you have sent gifts, some of you have sent an encouraging word and hundreds of you have prayed. I always knew Carol and I had friends but the love my family has been shown is just incredible. So I'm thankful for each and every one of you. I know some of you read my journal everyday but never comment. Please don't feel like you have to comment. This journal is more for me than it is for you anyway. He really does help me cope.

I'm sorry if this post is depressing this morning. I guess today I'm writing for me and not you. Yes you are welcome to read it, but I'm just writing down random thoughts. When you wake up in the middle of the night and can't get back to sleep, this is one thing that helps me cope. I have more I'd like to say but I'm just not ready to tell you all my thoughts and completely bare my soul to the world. I'm ready to come home and I'm ready to bring Carol home too. Hopefully that will happen soon. Carol's not done with her marathon yet and I don't know when she will be, but this morning I feel she can see the lift bridge in Canal Park. That will mean more to a few of you but most of you probably won't understand. Maybe you will someday but not today.

Bill

Day 33 Journal entry by Bill Funnemark — 11/21/2016

This morning I discovered a bunch of messages in my Messenger app from folks. I apologize for not responding sooner. I didn't know they were there. As some of you know or may have seen on Facebook this morning, Carol and I are coming home today. At least we are leaving today. Carol's first nurse here at Grand Strand Medical Center posted something about having a safe trip, so I guess everyone would soon know anyway. Carol is going by ground ambulance and should arrive at Good Samaritan Care Center in Algona Tuesday morning. I will probably not get there until Wednesday. I know a lot of people would like to come visit but I am requesting family only. Carol is still in a coma and would not know you were there anyway. This going to be a very private and stressful time for all us. So I just ask that you respect our family's wishes.

Bill

Day 34 Back Home Journal entry by Bill Funnemark — 11/22/2016

I just got a text from Mickolyn saying Carol is home. Her new home is not the house on N. Thorington but instead Algona Good Samaritan Care Center. This is the same facility she loved and hated for 30 years. As DON she would come home so often ready to cry. She wanted to quit more times than I could possibly count. She would be frustrated because two staff members were fighting, or someone didn't show up for work or someone just did something incredibly stupid in front of a state inspector. But every time I suggested she look for another job, Carol would have a thousand reasons why she couldn't leave. She really loved Good Sam and had such a passion for care of the elderly. She was tough on her employees but only because she wanted the best care for her beloved residents. Well now honey, you're going to get the best possible care any resident at Good Sam ever had. John will accept nothing less than the best for Carol. Thanks, Good Sam. I know you'll do a great job with my sweetheart.

I am quite a distance from home, however. I stopped at Spartanburg, SC last night. It took me a lot longer to get everything finished at Myrtle Beach than I had anticipated, and I was bone tired. I still have a really long day's drive or more likely day and a half, but family is there in Algona to watch over Carol. She's in good hands and she's in God's hands. Only God knows what lay ahead. He has a plan and whatever the plan is, we all will just have to accept it. I love to travel and most of my travels are alone on my motorcycle. The last few years Carol will fly to our destination while I ride, we meet up there, wherever there is, and enjoy each other's company. Today I'm taking a long solo journey but it's not much fun. I just want to be home. I'll be there soon.

Bill

Day 35 Home Journal entry by Bill Funnemark — 11/23/2016

I've had happier, more enjoyable trips from Myrtle Beach to Algona, but I am home, well not actually home, I'm at Good Samaritan. This will be Carol's home for the foreseeable future and my new home away from home. Mickolyn was here when Carol arrived on Tuesday morning and then Steph and her family arrived Tuesday evening. After a long drive and very little sleep I arrived in Algona around 11:15 this morning. It's kind of surreal to walk into this place knowing that Carol worked here for so many years. Some of her old staff have moved on, but many of her staff are still here and have made her so welcome. They are treating her like royalty. It is nice to be home but we all know Carol has a really tough road to travel yet. She's got to be somewhere in the 20 something mile area. We really don't know what to expect over the next few weeks, but I know she's in good hands.

I hope to be able to see some of you in the next few days or weeks since I'm home now. I know some of you would like to come visit Carol at

Good Sam, but for now we would like to restrict visitors to family. We just don't want to a steady parade of visitors. I want to be able to have my private time with Carol. I will be happy to get together with friends during my off hours, but I just ask that you respect our family's wishes. I know some of you just love reading my updates and that's great to know you appreciate my writing, but I don't know how much longer I will keep up with a daily entry. If there are changes in Carol's condition both positive and negative I will let everyone know but reporting each day that there are no changes will get a little old for you and me.

I plan to spend a little time with our family over the Thanksgiving weekend, so I will be taking a break from my daily vigil. But in my absence Carol will be in good hands with other family. I do have to say that I missed not waking up to the sounds and sights of the ocean the last couple mornings, but it is really good to be home. Happy Thanksgiving to all of you.

Bill

Day 36 Thanksgiving Journal entry by Bill Funnemark — 11/24/2016

Happy Thanksgiving to all of my followers. Today was a little different as you can imagine. Carol celebrated her Thanksgiving at Good Samaritan with some of our family coming and going. Each year we ask what we are thankful for. This last month has been really draining on me and my family, but I still have a lot to be thankful for. I'm thankful my family. With Carol's stroke I could feel bitter and feel sorry for myself, but I am so thankful to have all three of my children and six of my nine grandchildren here with me. It is rare to be able to get them together. We would have loved to have had the three granddaughters form Oregon here, but it just wasn't going to work. I am so thankful my extended family, siblings, in-laws, nieces, nephews and a few I have forgotten. I've had such tremendous support and help from so many of you. I am thankful for all my amazing friends. I've had so many kind words and deeds I can't enumerate them all. I don't have a lot more to say today, other than thank you to all of you.

Bill

Day 37 Black Friday Journal entry by Bill Funnemark — 11/25/2016

I'm not a big shopper and so I don't get super excited for Black Friday chaos. Our family spent Thanksgiving in Algona with family and visiting Carol at Good Sam. Then last night we all went to Mickolyn's house to unwind. Some of our crew did a little shopping a little after midnight, while I and a few others went to bed. We went to lunch today and then we split up to do a little low-key shopping. Will and I went to Bass Pro Shops to buy his belated birthday and premature Christmas present. After that I was pretty well shopped out, a good 30 minutes, and so Will and I went home. Carol has never been a big Black Friday shopper, but I think she enjoyed going with the girls to do a little Christmas preparation. Today is different though knowing I am with my family, spending some quality time with them, knowing Carol is lying in a bed in a nursing home in a coma. I know I have to continue living with some sense of normalcy but there isn't much normal about this holiday weekend. Carol is not alone. Her sister and a good friend were able to spend time with her at Good Samaritan today and tomorrow, giving me a couple days off. I am not complaining. I want to spend time with Carol, even if I'm just sitting there watching her or talking to her a little, but I need to get away a little and spend time with our family. I know Carol would not want me to spend my whole holiday just sitting with her. She would want me to enjoy my time with our kids and grandkids.

It's hard for me to think very seriously about Christmas these days. Carol has always been in charge of buying gifts for everyone. I just had to make sure I bought her one. But one of these days I will have to start thinking about this task. There are so many little details that Carol always just does, and I just have to show up. Well family, I'll apologize in advance just in case I forget to get your Christmas present. I'm going to need some serious Santa help this year. But for tonight I will just enjoy my family before they go back to Texas and Oregon or stays in Rhodes while I come back to Algona. Not back to what used to be, but instead back to my new normal for the foreseeable future. Hope you all had a great shopping day.

Bill

Day 38 Journal entry by Bill Funnemark — 11/26/2016

The dawn is just breaking as I sit down this morning to write. The first colors of dawn are appearing at the horizon and by the time I'm done with today's entry it will be full morning. Chad and Laura left about 5:30 to catch their flight back to Oregon. Steph, Pete, Connor, Daniel and Andrew left about 6:45 to start their drive back to Texas. I figured I might as well stay up since I couldn't go back to sleep anyway. I am sitting in the family room in Mickolyn's house while everyone else is sleeping, reflecting on all I have to be thankful for. You might question my thankfulness knowing my wife is lying in a coma for the 38th day, but I have so much to be thankful for.

I am thankful for the hundreds of friends and strangers who have been with me throughout this journey. I am thankful for your gifts, your prayers, for your acts of kindness and for your comments and words of support. I am thankful for my family, some whom I have not seen for a while and others I see on a regular basis. I am thankful for Jesus

Christ and that he loves me and promises to always be there for me. I am thankful that through Christ, Carol and I will never be apart for long. I am thankful for those who through my trials have been brought closer to their own families and to God. And I'm thankful for the Iowa State Cyclones, through the good times and the bad.

Carol seemed to respond a little to the presence of family and familiar surroundings. Whether these responses are meaningful or of any consequence I don't know. I do know that the longer she remains in a coma the more susceptible she will be to secondary problems like infections. With all of the wonderful advances in medical treatment that we have seen in the past few years, the brain still remains in large part a mystery. So we just wait and see what will happen today. If Carol makes it through today, we wait to see what tomorrow brings, and so on and so on. I just have to be patient. Hug your family and tell them you love them. Tomorrow may be too late. Happy birthday Mickolyn.

Bill

> Family Update:
> From: **Bill Funnemark**
> Date: Sat, Nov 26, 2016 at 6:52 AM
> Subject: Saturday Morning Update
>
> Happy birthday to my favorite middle daughter, Mickolyn. You have been a blessing to me for so many years. Trust me I know how many years, but I also know one has to be careful when revealing a woman's age. Thanksgiving is over, Black Friday has come and gone, and soon we will all be full into the Christmas season mode. But before I make that transition, I need to give thanks. I am truly blessed to know and count as friends, each and every one of you. You are included in this

email group because you are special. Some of you are actual family and some of you have been adopted into my family. Your official position is irrelevant. You are all special and I thank you for your support, whether it be through gifts of food, gift cards, cash, rides for me, hauling my kids from the airport, driving my car to South Carolina and then cooking real food for me, prayer support, a shoulder to cry on or just listening to me as a I try to cope with my reality these past 37+ days.

I think Carol had a good past few days as she made the transition from Grand Strand to Good Samaritan. The past couple days she seems to have responded to the presence of friends and family. She wiggled her toes for grandkids and sort of moved her eyes in what appeared to be an answer to a question. I don't know if these were real or not, but they sure seemed to be voluntary actions. As exciting as these actions were, the reality is that she is still in a deep coma and there are still many indications that she will never emerge from it. I don't know what the next few days will bring. It may bring more encouraging little steps forward, it may bring a steady decline, or it may bring status quo. Whatever happens I know without a doubt that Carol does not want to exist in this state. She is ready to go if her time is here and we, my children and I, are ready to let her go. This has been incredibly hard on everyone and Carol would be so saddened to know what she has put us through. This is not who she is or what she would ever want to do to us. I don't know if one can ever be ready to say goodbye, but I also want to do what is best for Carol. We moved Carol from Myrtle Beach to Algona and she is in hospice. Hospice is designed for end of life with dignity and compassion. I am not saying a miracle can't still happen, but it won't be very long before Carol will get an infection of some kind that her weakened body just won't be able to fight off.

I am thankful for many happy years of memories, friends and family. I am thankful that Carol believes in Christ and we will be together for eternity after she passes from this life. I am thankful for these last few weeks, as painful as they have been, but the blessings I have received from so many people has been just incredible. I am thankful that I can still enjoy my family. I am thankful to get the chance to visit Lorrie and Sam and enjoy their hospitality. I am thankful to be able to spend a little time with Nancy and your family. I am thankful for Denny and his words of encouragement both written and spoken. Yes, I have much to be thankful for this chilly Saturday morning. But with all of these things to be thankful for, I am still sad and I miss my Carol, the Carol I've known and loved for so many years. As the horizon is just turning color and the first few glimpses of dawn appear, I will close for today.

Dad/Bill/Mr. F

Day 39 Journal entry by Bill Funnemark — 11/27/2016

It's early Sunday afternoon here at Algona Good Samaritan. Carol is resting peacefully, I'm by her side watching the Cyclones play some basketball. Not a whole lot different than if we were at home. I'd be sitting in my recliner and Carol would probably be snoozing on the couch. The big difference of course is that if we were home she could go upstairs to bed where she'd be more comfortable or get up and get a cold Diet Dew to drink.

Thanksgiving is over and I'm back in Algona. This week I need to start getting my home routine going. When we were in Myrtle Beach, I had a daily routine. Most days I'd workout, eat a little breakfast and then go to the hospital. Then late in the afternoon or early evening I'd come back to our condo, eat a little dinner and go to bed. Now that I'm in Algona, the routine will be similar. Except now I can get caught up on the mail that's accumulated for the last 51 days. Most of the mail is junk thank goodness, but I suppose there might be a few important things there. In case anybody out there sent me a bill and I haven't paid it yet, I'm sorry. I'll get right on it. Another difference in my routine will be going to the Algona YMCA and no running on the beach. I can still run on the streets as long as we don't get a bunch of ice and snow. Which brings up another difference, Myrtle Beach doesn't get much snow. I suppose before long I will get to start blowing snow too. Boy am I excited about that. NOT.

Now that high school basketball season has started, I will be going to watch Will Clapper play. Hopefully the basketball team will have a good year and be competitive. Will has three games this week and depending on how Carol is doing, I will try to make some of them. Trice doesn't have any games until January and the Texas boys don't play until January either. Just a little bragging now. Will Clapper, a sophomore, was named 1st team all-district and 2nd team all-state as an offensive lineman. He was the only sophomore in all classes named to 2nd team or higher all state. Good job Will.

Life goes on.

Bill

Day 40 Journal entry by Bill Funnemark — 11/28/2016

Today has been a really hard day for me and I just don't have anything I can share tonight. Thank you for your understanding.

Bill

Day 41 Journal entry by Bill Funnemark — 11/29/2016

This will be somewhat brief, partly because there isn't a lot to report and partly because it's getting late. Everyone tells me I need to take a break and get away from the situation every so often. Today I did that. Our grandson Will had his first basketball game of the season tonight. So I drove down to Baxter, IA to watch. The CMB girls won their game but the boys didn't do so well. They played Greene County and they were hot from three-point land as well as everywhere else. Needless to say, it wasn't close. But Will played well and scored 23 points. It's only the first game of the season, so hopefully they can correct some problems and do better next game.

As for Carol, there is no improvement. This has been a common theme for 37 days now and each day it continues the prognosis gets worse. I know many of you are praying for a miracle and that Carol will wake up and be able to have some kind of quality life. The reality is that unless God does work some kind of miracle, recovery of any kind is just not going to happen. Her neurosurgeon told me before we left Myrtle Beach that there is very little hope for a recovery. And now it's been another week since we left there with no change. I have already told family and some close friends this and in more detail. I'm not going to share everything here though. I just want all of Carol's followers to know where we are right now. I ask you to continue to pray for Carol and the rest of our family. But I also want you to think about what to pray for. If this was your spouse or parent or even your child, would you want them to lie in a coma indefinitely? I don't know what is in store for Carol in the next few days or weeks, but my prayer is for God to take some kind of action. If she is to wake up and be at least partially who she was before, wonderful. If not, please take her home now.

Many of you have commented that you have an uncle or cousin or whatever who was in a coma for months and all of a sudden, they woke up and were more less fine. I don't doubt this. But there were probably signs that there was something going on in their brain. Or it was a totally different cause for the coma. I know you all mean well, but to be totally honest with you, at this point it doesn't really matter to me what happened to that person. I am struggling with my own situation and I'm pretty sure it is different than anything any of you have ever experienced. I hope no one takes this the wrong way or is offended by what I say here, that's not my intention. I just needed to vent a little. I welcome your prayers and comments and support. Somedays I just need to let my frustrations out of the bag a little.

Thank you everyone who reads my journal for your support. And it doesn't matter whether you post a comment or not, I still appreciate everything family, friends and strangers have done. I hope tomorrow I will be a little more upbeat.

Bill

Day 42 Journal entry by Bill Funnemark — 11/30/2016

I'm back in Algona sitting by Carol's side. No change in her condition. Some of you know some history about who Carol is but I'm sure many of you just know bits and pieces. So today I'm going to try to introduce you to Carol and give you some history. I have known Carol for as long as I can remember. We grew up in the same little town of Wesley, IA, we attended Sunday School and church at the Wesley Evangelical Free Church and we went to the same school. She lived in town and I lived on a farm. I suppose there was a time when I didn't know her, but as long as I can remember we were friends and classmates. We watched and cheered for each other in sporting events, she and her teams much more successful than I and my teams. We took many of the same classes together and had more or less the same circle of friends. When you go to a small school, graduating class of ~36, you know everyone. Even though we had always been friends we didn't date. That all changed about 50 years ago.

We both had dated other people, but we were both currently unattached. Corwith-Wesley always had a semi-formal dance in December. I had asked a different girl but got shot down, crushing my ego. So, I thought I could ask Carol. Since we had been friends for so long she might just take pity on me and say yes. Little did I know she'd had her eye on me for a long time. What did I know about love and girls? And the rest is history. I think Carol knew right away that I was the one for her. I on the other hand wasn't so sure about a long-term commitment, but I came around. Carol went off to nursing school after graduation and I went to Iowa State. Carol was born to be a nurse and loved her training and graduated in June 1970 at the top of her class. A month later we were married. I spent a year at ISU and decided instead of flunking out, getting drafted and winning a ticket to Vietnam, I would enlist in the Air Force. After leaving the USAF four years later and finishing my degree at ISU we moved to Algona. Carol eventually started working at Good Samaritan and 30 years later she retired on a Friday in January. The following Monday she began work as a nurse consultant, sharing her vast knowledge with many other facilities in Iowa.

That is just a very brief history of Carol's life.

Bill

This is an email I sent to family and a few close friends on November 30, 2016 at 8:14 A.M.

> Sorry for not keeping up with my duties!! Yesterday afternoon I drove down to Mickolyn's to watch Will's basketball game and time just got away from me. The game did not turn out so well.

CMB did hold their opponent to only 94. They had been on pace to score 140. First game of the season, so it gave the coach a lot to work with and Will scored 23.

Carol is still hanging on. I have discussed with her hospice nurse the possibility of shutting down the feeding tube but for the time being we have decided against that. I'm sure some of you might feel this wrong and that would be the same as starving Carol. There are very valid arguments on both sides of the issue and believe me, my kids and I have talked long and hard about this. For now, we agree to leave it in place. All of our discussions and the decisions we make may be a moot point. I was asking the nurse about the feeding tube and she said right now it is set at a rate that is correct for Carol's needs. However, her body is only letting in a very small amount and it appears that for some reason she is rejecting it. They are sure the machine is working, and the external line is fine but it may be plugged internally. It may be just blocked, or her body is doing something to block it. As long as the machine is working properly, I have instructed them to take no other action. She is being kept alive artificially anyway and if her body says no, I will respect that.

Carol did show some signs of responsiveness when the kids and grandkids were there at Thanksgiving, but nothing since. I don't know if there was just enough left of her that she was saving up for one last hurrah and now she's done or what. Several people said she did do definite movements in response to questions. I saw an eyebrow move once but that's about it. Of course, that's no surprise since she has not responded to me this whole time. She seems to save those things for our kids. That's ok Carol, but is it something I said? LOL I know I do things that irritate her at times, but she never holds a grudge this long. She thinks I'm too sweet for that kind of treatment and I know better than to argue with that kind of logic. Seriously though, I believe the family saw her respond even if I didn't. But there is no response now. She does not respond to voice, touch or pain. My Carol, my wife, my best friend, my lover, my partner is gone.

Love you all
Dad/Bill/Mr. F

Day 42/43 Non-Journal entry by Bill Funnemark — 11/30/-12/01/2016

This evening I met some friends at Flipside in LuVerne, IA for pizza and companionship. I spent time during the day at Carol's side, but took some time off for myself. I got back to Algona around 8:00 P.M. but just couldn't face going to my empty house and I just didn't want to go to Good Sam. I decided to visit my friends Pam and Denny. I drop in on them at all hours of the day, early morning for coffee or evening for conversation. We talked for a little while and sometime after 9:00 P.M. I got a call from Good Sam that Carol had taken a turn. There had been a definite change. I remember saying to Pam and Denny, "Thank God. I think this might be over." Denny called my pastor and I think I called Mickolyn. I don't know if I called Steph and Chad or not. I probably did, but I don't remember.

Mickolyn packed a few things and headed to Algona and arrived sometime after midnight. I had told her and the rest of the family that Carol's condition had changed and I didn't know how long she would be with us or if she'd even be alive when Mickolyn got here. She made it. Steph caught the first flight she could get but the earliest she would arrive in Des Moines was later in the afternoon. One of Steph's best friends, Mary Lee called her sister Liz who just happened to be in Des Moines. Liz drove to the airport, picked up Steph at the curb and raced to Algona. Evidently no police were in the area and no speeding tickets were issued.

Carol's sisters and their families gathered at Good Sam, while Mickolyn and I kept vigil. Both of us were exhausted but didn't want to leave. Our Hospice nurse, Serena, very professionally cleared the room so the two of us could rest in Carol's room. Steph arrived early evening. We kept updating her as she rode along but couldn't say if Carol would still be alive when she got here. So, by now most of the family had gathered at Good Sam except for Chad. Since he and Laura had just been here, they really didn't think they could afford to turn around and fly right back, especially since he couldn't get here in time. We set up a video chat on a laptop computer so he and his family could be with us for these last few minutes or hours.

Everyone got to say their good-byes to Mom/Grandma/sister/aunt and wife. Carol's temperature had been fluctuating for the last couple days and we thought she may have contracted an infection. Her doctor said, "No there is no infection. The portion of her brain that regulates temperature is shutting down." Her pulse slowed, respirations became weaker and weaker, oxygen saturation began to drop and her blood pressure became so weak that it couldn't be measured. Carol was just hanging on and was just not ready to give up. Finally, Serena asked if we had told Carol that Chad was not actually here at Good Sam. Mickolyn and Steph told their mom that Chad and his family were still in Oregon but watching on the computer. He would not be able to be here physically and it is okay to let go. In less than five minutes, she breathed her last. It was over.

Day 43 The Race is Run Journal entry by Bill Funnemark — 12/1/2016

Carol has passed the 26-mile marker and is in the home stretch. She can see the finish line a mere 0.2 miles ahead. What's at the finish line you might ask? In a real marathon, you get a medal, maybe a rose for the women and a bottle of water. For Carol, it is the gates of Heaven.

She will be getting so much more than some old medal. Jesus will be there to greet her with her very own crown. When I started running many years ago, I started with 5K races, then 10K and eventually full marathons. Carol was at every race I ever ran cheering me on. In the shorter races, she would wait for me at the finish line. But on the longer ones like marathons she and usually a few passengers would tear around the city looking for a vantage point to offer me words of encouragement like, "Looking good Bill" or "Way to go" or "You're almost there." And then she'd race to the finish line to cheer me on at the end. It didn't matter how fast or slow I'd run, she was always there with "Looking good, go for it, Babe."

Well Carol knows we both have our own marathons to run. Our finish line is Heaven. So of course, she had to get there before me. If she didn't, who would cheer and yell "Looking good Babe. Way to go. You're almost there."

"For I am already being poured out as a drink offering, and the time of my departure has come. I have fought the good fight, I have finished the race, I have kept the faith. Henceforth there is laid up for me the crown of righteousness, which the Lord, the righteous judge, will award to me on that day, and not only to me but also to all who have loved his appearing." (2 Timothy 4:6-8 ESV)

On December 1, 2016, at about 8:13 PM Carol completed her marathon and is now cheering with Jesus and waiting for me to join her. I love you so much Carol and I will miss you every day until we are reunited in Heaven. I will not say good-bye, but instead AufWiedersehen (auf vee der sayen), which means "Until We Meet Again". I love you Carol.

Bill

Day 44 Funeral Arrangements Journal entry by Stephanie Hamell — 12/2/2016

Visitation will be December 11th at Grace Church, Algona, IA (First Baptist Church) 4:30-8:00 pm with the funeral Monday the 12th at 10:30 am at Grace as well.

Day 44 Some Last Thoughts Non-Journal entry by Bill Funnemark — 12/02/2016

These next few paragraphs were not ever posted on Carol's Caring Bridge site. At the time I wrote these words, it was just too fresh and personal to share with the whole world. I didn't even share these words with my family. But now on January 1st, I feel that it is ok to share them. These words were written around 1:42 the morning following Carol's death.

These past several weeks have been just unbelievable. One minute we're having a fun lunch with good friends looking out at the ocean and the next minute my life changes forever. I knew I had lost the Carol. I knew within a few minutes of her getting sick. I could tell it was more than a bad upset stomach. But when I got to the hospital they didn't have a record of her yet. She was already being worked on someplace, but her paperwork hadn't caught up with her yet. I asked again about her condition and the lady at the desk called someone and then told me to come to this consultation room. I knew that didn't sound good. I sat there forever it seemed like before an ER doctor came into talk to me. When he said "I'm sorry (not a reassuring first line) but your wife had a massive brain bleed, is stable now but in very critical condition," I just lost it. It was like getting kicked in the teeth, then in the stomach and then for good measure a good swift kick to the nuts. And that was just the beginning.

When I got a call Wednesday night, November 30th, that she had taken a turn for the worse, I was sad but also so relieved. At that point I knew Carol would never wake up or if she did, she would be nearly a vegetable. I just wanted her to give up and die. We all were at the point where death was a true blessing for everyone. I thought I'd be ok when it finally happened, but I was wrong. I had some very special, intimate moments with Carol through this whole trip. Especially in Myrtle Beach, there were many days that I spent several hours alone with Carol just sitting in her hospital room. There would be nurses and other staff coming and going, but their visits were usually brief. I can't tell my kids some of this because they would think it was weird, especially coming from their dad. But for some reason I can tell you.

Carol and I had a really, good marriage and we enjoyed each other's company. We had a good sex life too, especially for a couple of old people. I would rub her arm or her hands, or if I was sure no one was going to be popping in the door, I would caress her breasts hoping for any kind of reaction. Nothing. That really hurt to know, although I was trying to be so gentle and kind with her, she was totally ignoring me. She wouldn't even frown or scowl at me and she certainly displayed no pleasure. I tried to pinch her really hard in various places where I'd seen the doctors do the same thing trying to get a response and I got nothing. This happened very early, probably from day four on. I tried to be kind and gentle and I tried to be rough, within reason, and nothing gave any response. I knew then there was nothing left of Carol at that point, but I just kept hoping.

Wednesday night, when Good Sam called me to let me know Carol had taken a turn for the worse, I was happy and sad. Happy that the end of this horrible journey was a little closer to being over but sad for the same reason. As the evening progressed and she got weaker and weaker, the realization that she was actually going to die started to really sink in. I prayed for her to hang on just two more hours, so she would still be alive when Mickolyn got there. Then I went through the same process while waiting for Stephanie to get there. Just hang on until 3:30 so Steph can say goodbye, again. Then we went through it again waiting for her sister Barb. It was excruciating to be pleading with my best friend, wife, lover and mother of my children to just hang on for another 30 minutes. Each time she did.

At one point during the day on Thursday there were several of Carol's side of the family there, all crammed into her room. I know they just wanted to spend time with her but Mickolyn and I were getting annoyed. When two hospice nurses asked if we needed anything, I said yes. You can ask all these people to leave. Mickolyn and I were exhausted and needed to rest. So, they very discretely got rid of them so Mickolyn and I could take a little cat nap but still be by Carol's side. I don't know if she knew we were there. I doubt she did, but we knew. I sat for hours at a time just holding Carols hand, stroking her arm and caressing her breasts just like everything was normal and we were lying in our own bed at home. Except we were in a nursing home and she felt nothing. There was nothing sexual about it, just the familiar touch of my lover's body.

Usually, whenever staff came to move Carol or do some treatment, they would chase everyone from the room. But one evening, two hospice workers came in to give Carol a bath. I didn't feel like getting up and leaving the room. So, I asked if I could just stay. I informed them that I had seen Carol naked before and I'd watched staff both here at Good Sam and in Myrtle Beach clean her trach tube, so it didn't really matter. One of the most intimate acts I have ever witnessed was to watch them as they gently and lovingly washed Carol and then rubbed her down with lotion. Again, there was nothing sexual about it, even watching them wash and lotion her breasts. The entire procedure just soothed me and made me incredibly sad. Here is the woman who has been my partner for five decades and soon to be just an empty shell. And these two hospice workers knew full well that Carol would very soon be dead, but they treated her so kindly and gently. It was just an incredible few moments that I will never forget, but I'm not sure I can ever share it with my children. At least I don't think I can share it to the degree I have with you.

I said earlier that I thought I was prepared for those last moments because I'd already gone through about ever emotion I thought I could. I had cried all the tears I possibly could. I would be relieved to know Carol was no longer trapped in the shell of human being. Happy to know Carol was in Heaven. But when those last few breaths came, and we knew it was almost over, I just couldn't hold back, not that I'd been very successful at it before. It was hard to know whether she was breathing or not because her breaths were so shallow. You couldn't find a pulse in her wrists but there was a little flicker in one spot on her neck. But then that stopped too. The nurse came in and listened with a stethoscope, turned to me, shook her head and said, "I'm sorry, she's gone." It was 8:13 P.M., December 1, 2016. I just cried like a baby. All the raw emotion that I had been trying to keep somewhat in check just let loose. It was just awful. As I sat there and just stared at my beautiful wife, hair all chopped off, tube sticking out of her neck and knowing she was really, finally dead was just more than I could handle.

After a time of mourning for those of us in the room, the nurse came and cleaned her up a little, removed the breathing tube and tried to make her look as good as possible. The Good Sam staff had a short memorial service and then gradually everyone left except Stephanie, Mickolyn and me. Chad had been there all afternoon via a video chat but not in person. Finally, it was just Carol and me in the room, no one else. Carol was already starting to cool, and her face was as pale as pale could be. I knelt beside her bed, held her cold hand, talked to her empty shell of a body, prayed something and just wept. I couldn't bring myself to leave. It wasn't creepy or weird, it just seemed so natural. It was then that it really hit me that Carol, my wife, the mother of my babies, my best friend, my lover, my all, was really gone and my life was going to be completely changed forever.

I said good-bye, grabbed the pizza box with a few pieces left in it, and walked out. It struck me later how pathetic I must have looked, walking down the hall carrying a pizza box, feeling as alone as I'd ever felt in my life. I don't know what happened after that. I must have gone home to my empty bed, to my empty house, to my empty life.

I will survive. I will stop crying at random moments. I will be happy again. But I will never be the same.

Day 45 Post Marathon Thoughts Journal entry by Bill Funnemark — 12/03/2016

Carol's marathon ended peacefully around 8:13 PM on December 1, 2016. After I would run a marathon, I would find it hard to even walk. Every muscle in my body would be tired, but my legs especially would ache. You could recognize others who ran the race by the way they shuffled along the street. After some marathons I would actually feel pretty good, knowing I could have gone farther if I really wanted to, but why would I want to. One year, Mickolyn and I ran the Des Moines Marathon together. We stayed together for a while, but she was just not feeling it that day and began to lag behind. She insisted that I keep going and she'd see me at the finish line. I did finish and was doing my normal slow walk around the finish area when she called me. She was about three miles from the finish line and was really struggling. So, what do you do when you really love someone and that someone needs help? You go help them. I ran back to meet her, and we sort of ran to the finish line together. Had I not been with her at the end, I'm not sure she would have finished. I ran about 29 miles that day, farther than I have ever gone. I don't know how I could have done that, but from somewhere deep inside I found the strength to carry on.

I know where Carol got her strength to carry on. It came from God. In those last few hours Carol's breathing was so weak and shallow, and her blood pressure was so low we couldn't understand how she could keep going. I sat in a chair beside her bed holding her hand. Steph and Mickolyn were beside her and her two sisters and her brother-in-law were there too. My laptop computer was resting on Carol's stomach with Chad connected via a video chat from Oregon. We were all sobbing not wanting to let her go but, yet we wanted her struggle to end. We wanted her to go home to be with Jesus, but she just wouldn't give up. Finally, our hospice nurse asked if Carol knew that Chad was not actually coming to Good Sam? He was there through the video chat but physically he was still in Oregon with has girls. Within two minutes of telling Carol this she finished her race. I guess she just couldn't quite make it to the finish line without a little help.

Some of you who have been following Carol's journey through me have never experienced the death of a really close loved one. I lost my mother when I was only 22 after her battle with cancer and I lost my dad only a few years ago. And I have lost many other relatives and friends over the years, but nothing has ever been as beautiful and painful as losing my beloved Carol. She was my wife, the mother of my children, my lover and my best friend. After she had died and after the brief memorial service that Good Samaritan did in her honor, everyone left the room and it was just me and my best friend. And even as her body began to cool and turn pale, I just couldn't bear to let her go. I needed some help to make to the finish line too. Carol, by that time, already with Jesus, must have asked Him to please help me make it through the next few minutes, few hours, few days, few years. I am ok but I miss my friend, but I will see you again someday.

This may be my last entry on Caring Bridge or it might not be. At some point this too must end. I will just see what the next few days bring.

Bill

Day 46 Journal entry by Bill Funnemark — 12/04/2016

Some of you who have been following Carol's marathon don't want me to quit writing. I have seen in your comments that you want to hear more. I plan to keep adding some updates but not every day. For one thing, there is not that much to say anymore. Carol provided me great material to write about. There were many days of just sitting and watching but with not much action. Then there were days when major events occurred, like the morning we both left Myrtle Beach. The same goes for after her death. The next few days will be busy for me as I prepare for my new life. There are the obvious things to be done, like attend to funeral arrangements, find pictures for Carol's tribute, make sure my suit is clean and I have a clean shirt to wear. I sure hope my dress shirt is clean and pressed. I can wash clothes, but it's been a long time since I've done any ironing. T-shirts and sweatshirts don't require that degree of care.

I suppose there are some legal type stuff I will need to address. I need to contact Carol's life insurance company, her Medicare supplement company and those kinds of people. I need to try to find a home for the box of Longaberger baskets that just arrived at my house. I haven't even opened the box and have no idea if they are Carol's or if she ordered them for someone else. If they are for someone else, good luck with finding the rightful owner. I still have Carol's luggage from vacation, not even opened, to go through and do something with. Carol has her work computer and printer, procedures manuals and confidential correspondence that needs to be destroyed or returned to Gwen.

In the next few weeks I will have plenty to do and most of it won't be all that exciting or news worthy. I don't think I need to share with the world that "Oh today I hauled a semi load of clothes to Goodwill." Obviously, Carol's visitation next Sunday, December 11th will be all consuming. I have been to these things as a visitor like many of you will be, but I've also been involved as a participant like when my mother died. I just remember it was a long tiring process for me, a young man (age 22), still a new husband (2 years), fairly new father (8 months) and a recently discharged Air Force veteran and now college student (2 months). I didn't know how to act or what to say. I met lots of people, some I knew but many I didn't and stood around for hours. This time will be different. This time my whole life will be different.

I will keep writing as I have things to say but it probably won't be daily.

Bill

Day 47 Journal entry by Bill Funnemark — 12/5/2016

I know I should be in bed but I'm not tired. It seems my internal clock is out of whack. So, I thought I might as well write a little. This past weekend I just left town after tending to a little business. On Friday Steph, Mickolyn and I met with my pastor and the funeral director to work out details for Carol's upcoming funeral which is a week from now. Visitation is Sunday, December 11th and the funeral is Monday, December 12th. Arrangements are being handled by Lentz Funeral Home of Algona.

So many people have offered to do things for me and my family, that it is a bit overwhelming. I know people mean well and I have actually taken a few people up on their offers of help. I don't want to sound ungrateful at all, but I really don't need anything right now, especially food. I have plenty of food. I am not going hungry. I have probably put on 10 pounds since this all started. It's not that I don't want your food, it's just that I have plenty right now. I can't eat what I already have before it goes bad. I will be spending a lot of time visiting my daughter's home and going to basketball games. If I have too much stuff at my house, it will just go to waste. I don't plan to have people to my house for dinner and my dietary requirements are pretty simple.

I really do appreciate the offers but please don't bring me food. If you feel you must cook something, take it to a family who really needs it or donate the money you would have spent on me to the Algona Good Samaritan Foundation. This is the charity that my family and I have designated for memorial gifts to go to. You can either send the money to Good Samaritan with a note to let them know what it is for, send it to Lentz Funeral Home in Algona or send it to me and I will make sure it gets there. This foundation purchases extra things for the nursing home to help improve the residents' quality of life. Carol donated to the Good Sam Foundation every time one of her residents died and we are just caring on the tradition. We are also asking that instead of spending money on flowers, you give the money to the Foundation.

I know many of you who have been following my Caring Bridge posts have also contributed to our GoFundMe account or sent me money directly. Originally this fund was established because we thought the only way to get Carol home was by air ambulance which would have cost about $18,000 and Medicare would not pay a dime. But the fund was also supposed to help me with Carol's other medical expenses. I have no idea how much all of this will cost me. Carol had insurance but it's way too early for any of those bills to have been processed. Our intention is to donate whatever funds we have left after paying our medical related expenses to the Good Sam Foundation.

I know the remarks above are a lot different than most of my previous journal entries, but that's what's on my mind early Monday morning. One item I wanted to share though that isn't of mundane day to day stuff is a song I sang as a solo in church many years ago. At the time I sang it, it was just a song. It was not about me or anyone in particular. When I finished singing this song that morning almost the entire congregation was drying their eyes. Oops, I didn't mean to do that. I hadn't thought about this song in many years until a couple days ago when Chad asked me the name of it. He remembered the song but didn't know the name of the artist who performed it. The song is "This Time It's Different/Does Jesus Care" by Steve and Annie Chapman. It talks about an old man who leaves the hospital one last time but this time he leaves alone. I have been to the hospital many times over the years, never as a patient, but to visit Carol at the birth of our children or when one of them was sick or when Carol had surgery or something. But this time I left without my sweetheart. Listen to this song and see if you can maybe get a tiny glimpse of my pain.

As painful as this whole ordeal has been, there are times when you just have to laugh. Today after making funeral arrangements, Mickolyn, Stephanie and I went to Mickolyn's home for the weekend. Will had a basketball game at Roland-Story and we all went to it to support him and to just try to forget about everything for a few hours. The game didn't go well and CMB lost. I had not seen Will since Carol had died and I didn't have an opportunity to talk to him before the game. He is always the last person out of the locker room, win or lose and tonight was no exception. We're all standing around the foyer waiting for him along with a few people from Roland-Story. As Will walked in, I walked up to him to give him a hug. He burst into tears, as did I. Afterwards Courtney said, "I bet those people must think you really took that loss hard!" We all burst into laughter and tears. Thanks Courtney, we needed that.

Bill

Imagine Journal entry by Chad Funnemark — 12/5/2016

I have yet to make it through this song in the last 47 days with dry eyes. A great friend shared this with us today, and I thought I'd do the same. At least my mom doesn't have to imagine any longer. "I Can Only Imagine" by MercyMe.

Day 48 Journal entry by Bill Funnemark — 12/6/2016

I have spent a good share of the last few days working on details for Carol's funeral, meeting with some dear friends and going to basketball games. I think my parts of funeral arrangements are done. Now it's up to the professionals to put everything together. One chore that was a lot easier than I thought it would be was picking a cemetery plot. Carol is going to be cremated and when my time comes, so will I. I learned that on a standard sized plot you can bury two urns, so I only needed one plot. There was a plot available directly behind the graves of Carol's parents and that seemed like as good a place as any. The task was really very easy.

You might wonder why Carol's body is being cremated and that's a valid question. One reason is that one of my children just doesn't like the idea of people looking at her dead body. That was actually reason enough but there are others. I have been to many funerals in my life as have most mature (old) people like me. I always feel obligated to stand by the coffin and stare at the departed loved one and then move on. I hear people say, "Oh doesn't Uncle Joe or cousin Mary look so good?" No, he/she is dead. They don't look all that good. It is a dead body and no matter how hard the funeral people try; the person still looks dead.

Another more personal reason we are having Carol's body cremated is that she didn't look like the Carol all of you know. She had two holes drilled in her head, a shunt put in, hair shaved off and she just didn't look the way I wanted people to remember her. Some of my family and a very few non-family members saw Carol while she was at Good Samaritan, but the vast majority of her friends did not. The way she looked didn't bother me in the least because I had much greater concerns, but out of respect for my best friend, I didn't want others to see her like that. I got in trouble one night because we had ridden somewhere, I think to the Flipside in LuVerne, with the top down and I neglected to tell her that her hair was a little windblown. I didn't make that mistake again.

We plan to bury most of Carol's ashes in our plot here in Algona. But I am saving a few ashes to carry with me on my motorcycle and sometime when I get back to the beach, I plan to spread a few at one her favorite spots in this beautiful country, the ocean. It doesn't really matter though, because Carol is in Heaven now. What is left here on Earth is just part of her body. It isn't her. I will always have Carol's memory with me. It doesn't matter if her body was buried in an expensive box or her ashes in a beautiful urn, she is not here anyway.

On a little lighter note dealing with cremation, I must share how one of my younger grandchildren described the process. "They put Grandma in a box and burn her up and then dump her ashes in a jar." I guess that's the general idea but maybe a little work on terminology is in order. And on that note, I'm going to bed.

Bill

Day 50 Journal entry by Bill Funnemark — 12/8/2016

Today was a busy day for me. I got a good start on my list of tasks that need to be done. Tasks like contacting Carol's life insurance company, contacting IPERS, cancelling her dental insurance and many other tasks that I haven't even thought of yet. I went to the Algona Family YMCA this morning for a simple hour workout, figuring I'd be out of there by 8:30. But that was not to be. So many friends, some I've known for many years, and some I only see at the Y and they all wanted to talk to me. I really had no place I had to be, so I just talked and listened and continued to heal.

I know some of my friends have been afraid to contact me because they didn't know what to say or didn't want to bother me. I understand this, I was the same way. But trust me, it's ok to speak. I have a friend who I played softball against for many years when I moved to Algona. I always considered him a friend, not someone I'd go out to dinner with or have over to my house, but we were, and I hope still are friends. For years I'd see him and his wife at the Y. I knew what machines they each would use, and I'm sure knew the same about me. My friend came down with ALS and slowly he lost more and more control of his body, and eventually he couldn't come to the Y anymore, but his wife is there on a regular basis. I have hesitated for too long to ask her how her husband is doing these days or even if he was still even alive. This morning while one Carol consoled me on the loss of my Carol I realized I was doing the same thing as many of my friends are doing. I was afraid to ask her how her husband is getting along, was he still alive even. Just like in my life, she shared with me about my friend. I'm sorry Carol for not asking sooner.

It is hard to know what to say, but don't be afraid. Call, text, email or even video chat while in bed with your friend. Your friend just wants to hear from you. I will try to do a better job.

After I finished my tasks this morning, I needed to go up town to do a few more errands. I had had a good morning. I was busy and hardly even thought of how much I missed my best friend. As I was driving out of my yard the song "Different Kind of Christmas" by Mark Schultz came on. It talks about how Christmas will be different this year with one less plate at the table and so on. I just had to stop, dry my eyes so I could see where I was going, and then drive on to the bank. It is supposed to be getting easier and I guess it is, but everyday there seems to be another memory that just sneaks up and smacks me upside the head. Every little kindness that friends have shown me sure helps though. I just can't thank you enough.

Bill

Day 52 Journal entry by Bill Funnemark — 12/10/2016

Tonight is the night before Carol's visitation and why wouldn't it be snowing? We haven't had any snow since last spring and of course the weekend when people will be traveling to visit our family, we have the first winter storm of the season. My children and grandchildren had planned to all meet at Mickolyn's, go to Will's basketball game this afternoon and then drive to Algona in the morning. I told my kids that their appearance, although expected was not mandatory in case of bad weather. I on the other hand had to be there. So, I drove home this morning, so I would be sure to miss any severe weather. Steph and her boys are here as well as Chad and his family. Mickolyn and her family and Denny, my brother, are on their way to Algona too. I'm doing pretty well, all things considered but I know I will have some tough times over the course of the few days. We had picked out a couple really nice pictures of Carol to have blown up for a display at visitation. As Chad was putting them in the back of the car I just caught a glimpse of them. Even though I knew what they were, just seeing her again about did me in.

I am trying to prepare myself for tomorrow afternoon but am wondering if I can hold it together. One minute I am fine and the next I'm not. I know when I see some people at the church I will be fine. I will be able to talk semi-intelligently without a lot of emotion. But the next person coming up to me will bring a totally different reaction. I know when I see a certain, few individuals I will lose it though and it may not be the ones who I think it will be. I am ready to have this all over with and move on, but I also can hardly bare to close this door on our lives. I know I am not the first man to ever lose his wife and I won't be the last, but this is the first time for me and I'm just not sure how I'm supposed to handle everything.

Last Sunday as I drove Steph to the airport in Minneapolis I asked her what the proper etiquette was for wearing your wedding band after your wife dies. I have no plans to remove my ring, I would feel naked without it, but I just wondered. I usually do things my own way without regard for what is expected. I tend to do things my own way, as some of you may have noticed. That is one of the beautiful things about Carol's and my marriage. Often when we went on vacation, she would fly, and I would ride my motorcycle to our destination. It's not that we didn't like to travel together because we did plenty of that too. Carol knew how much I enjoyed a long bike trip and encouraging me to go for a ride was just one of her simple acts of kindness and love. Almost everything she ever did in her life was for someone else. Even when she would splurge and get her nails done, it was more for me than it was for herself.

Oh Carol, as this final day draws near, I just miss you so much. I know you have touched the heart of so many through your many years of service, but I just want you back. I love you so much Babe.

Bill

Day 54 Journal entry by Bill Funnemark — 12/12/2016

This weekend has been a whirlwind of activity and emotions and in a few hours for the most part it will be over. I have family coming in from all parts of the country. I've had grandkids meeting for the first time ever, cousins meeting other cousins, CWL students meeting my family and finally putting a face to each other. Both have heard about the others but had either never met or it had been many years. Last night at the visitation I wasn't sure what to expect. I knew I would cry at times but just wasn't sure when. I got there early, and the funeral director got there early too and started the slide show. As I sat there all alone in the sanctuary watching memories flash by on the screen I couldn't help but smile at times, remembering a happy occasion, a ride with the top down, a picture of food, one of the grandkids. But then would flash up a picture of Carol, looking so beautiful and I would just start crying to myself. Slowly others of my family started to arrive, but the sanctuary remained solemnly quiet except for an occasion laugh or cry. These few slides were just a snippet of Carol's life.

As the guests started to file into the church and past our little greeting line, we would hear short stories about Carol or how she had impacted someone's life or some good deed she'd done. I was reunited with her best friend from high school, a lady who Carol hadn't actually seen in nearly 50 years and until very recently with the help of Facebook, hadn't spoken either. But yet it was like we were still in high school and had only been a part for a few weeks. We asked each other, "Why did we wait so long to get together?" Neither of us had an answer. Why do we allow dear friends to simply drift apart? I know we all get busy with our own families, but our friends are important too. I guess I need to make one of those vows to try to do a better job.

The whole visitation process was draining but it was so nice to see so many of our friends. A few people were total strangers to me until they introduced themselves and then in most cases I knew who they were. I'll admit though, that even after introductions I didn't have a clue. And of course, a few I knew very well but drew a total blank at their name when introduction time came. Sorry if I missed your name. For one young lady, former student, it took until this morning, but the name finally came to me. But even if I forgot your name at the moment, I still thank you for coming to show respect for my best friend. Carol would have been humbled and probably a little embarrassed by all the fuss over her, but trust me Babe, you deserved every bit of praise to come your way last night.

I planned to get a really good night's sleep, so I would be fresh for the funeral today. I left the hotel where most of my family is staying and came home to go to bed. I was tucked snuggly in bed by 10:15, went right to sleep and was able sleep all the way to 3:00 AM. but trying to go back to sleep wasn't working so well. So, after a futile attempt to rest I got up and went to the YMCA for an early morning workout. I think I will have enough emotions on hand to keep me awake during the funeral and a brief step outside should shock me awake if need be. In a way I am looking forward to the funeral later this morning. A celebration of Carol's life and a testament of her love of God and family. But this is also the last stage of her incredible journey, one I've been able to share with her for so long. This part of our journey on Earth is about to come to an end, but I will join you again someday for eternity. Until that day I miss you Carol and I will always love you. OK. I can do this.

Bill

Day 55 Journal entry by Bill Funnemark — 12/13/2016

After a good night's sleep, I'm ready to face the day after. What began around 1:15 PM on October 20, 2016 with a hemorrhagic stroke, a massive brain bleed, ended with a beautiful funeral on December 12. 2016. During the countless hours of sitting by Carol's side, speaking to doctors, praying for Carol's recovery and later praying that she could just go Home, loss of sleep, hugs and kisses from family friends and total strangers, my family and I have crossed so many milestones. And you, our many friends have been right there for us the whole time. Yesterday was the culmination of this journey, sort of like the awards ceremony following the marathon. Of course, I never finished high enough in any marathon to ever appear on the podium. I don't know what it's really like, I can only imagine. (That would be a good name for a song.)

Many of my journal junkies attended Carol's funeral yesterday but even more of you did not. Carol was never about her, she was always thinking about others, it's a nurse thing. When I would ask her, "Where would you like to go eat for your birthday?" The response would always be, "Oh I don't care, where do you want to go?" Her whole life was about serving others. She would do about anything for her family, even me, if it was remotely possible. She would alter her vacation plans in order to accommodate her consultation clients. She served her Lord and Savior in her own way. Pastor Peter pointed out in his message how Carol prayed often and praised God for every little thing in her life. The funeral yesterday glorified God and pointed out to everyone who was there how Carol lived her life in God's will.

Many tears were shed before, during and after the service. Many kind words were spoken. And a lot of hugs were shared. But at the end of the day, Carol's ashes are in the ground, flowers have been dispersed, cards and pictures brought home, family have started to go back to their own homes and the other side of my bed is very empty. Kind words and lots of hugs just don't take the place of being able to share my life with my wife, best friend and lover. I will get used to my new life, but I still miss Carol in so many ways. As I move forward, I hope no one thinks I am forgetting her. I will grieve in my own way, just like I did almost everything in my life, my own way. If you see or hear of me driving around the country in our little Audi TT or riding on my Triumph, please don't think I'm throwing Carol's memory to the side. She will be riding with me. Carol's funeral was a beautiful ceremony. Pastor Peter did an awesome job of pulling everything together. Our dear friend AJ did an amazing job with her music. Her love for Carol was obvious as she struggled to sing the final few words of her song. There was no act there, just true love for a friend she will never see again in this life. Thank you to everyone who had a part in the day. You made a very hard situation tolerable. And now it is the day after. I guess it is time to get started with it.

Bill

Day 58 Journal entry by Bill Funnemark — 12/16/2016

It's been a couple days since it wrote anything and some of you are probably going through Caring Bridge withdrawal. The last few days have been busy at times but with plenty of down time. I spent most of my time going through sympathy cards. It is so nice to know that Carol had so many friends, but it does make for a lot of cards. I will be working on mailing thank you cards but don't expect them for a few days. The adjustment to being single is a work in progress and it's mostly going ok. I have tried to maintain some sort of schedule, go to the YMCA, run a few errands around town, go home and work on cards or other funeral related tasks, eat a little breakfast somewhere in there and then maybe some supper and then a quiet evening watching TV by myself. Staying busy during the day helps the time go by and to take my mind off my sorrow. But in the quiet times I have trouble keeping my mind off the past.

I also keep finding new tasks. A simple job like reconciling my Quicken points out a couple reoccurring charges that I never really paid any attention to. Carol and I shared almost everything in our lives, but we didn't always share all the details. I didn't always tell her how much it cost to service my motorcycle or buy new tires for it and she had a few not so secret, secrets, like how much she spent at the beauty shop. I don't think I need to keep paying for her online Weight Watchers account although I maybe should have changed the name to Bill instead of cancelling it. So, along with many other tasks, I had to figure out how to cancel her membership.

As I go through my daily routine, I run into friends and acquaintances who have also lost a loved one. Some I barely know, others I've dealt with for years but never really knew them and others who are really good friends. Sharing their memories or their thoughts does help, losing a spouse is so different. My mother died at the age of 49, just a couple months after I was discharged from the Air Force, and although that was hard, it was nothing like losing my wife. I was only 22 years old. Carol and I were married for over 46 years. So, I knew her more than twice as long as I knew my own mother. I know the relationship between mother and son is completely different than husband and wife, but I just want to point out that I knew a whole lot more about Carol than I ever did about my mother. As I visit with folks who have lost a spouse, I am hopeful that I too will be happy again and I can be content with my life again. It's not fair, but that's just the way life is.

I realized yesterday that Christmas is very near. I know it's December and that today is the 16th, but it never really occurred to me that I need to do some Christmas shopping. That was Carol's job. I of course had the job of shopping for her gift and I helped shop for the rest of the family, but it was always Carol who had the list. I'm afraid my kids and grandkids will be getting mostly gift cards this year unless Santa steps up big time. It's just another one of those tasks that needs to be done.

Bill

Day 60 Journal entry by Bill Funnemark — 12/18/2016

The Firsts begin. It has been six days since Carol's funeral and almost two months since Carol's journey began. I have had many people tell me how hard the first year is going to be. There is the first Christmas, the first anniversary, the first birthday and so many other firsts. This morning they began. On my way to church I stopped at Kum & Go to get my cappuccino, no Diet Dew, and everything was fine. But as I walked into church, all of a sudden it hit me, Carol's not with me. I sat in my normal spot, 2nd row from the back, aisle seat. It seemed a little empty, but it was still ok. Then we started singing and of course we sang traditional Christmas songs, including "The First Noel", my favorite. Carol loved the Christmas season and she loved the old, traditional Christmas carols. Needless to say, I had a little trouble singing all the words. A very dear friend saw me struggling and came over and gave me some comfort. And then near the end of the service the pastor had to mention the empty chair and the implications. Thanks a lot Pastor Peter for triggering the tears again. One First down, many more to go.

Bill

Day 62 Journal entry by Bill Funnemark — 12/20/2016

It's great to have friends, some just acquaintances, others very dear, but you are all important. Last night I had a wonderful evening with a couple in the very dear category. We had a nice meal and several hours of great conversation. It helps to be able to talk to people and to be able to share in my healing process. There are some things I can talk about with family, some things with certain friends, but there are some things you can only talk about with a very few. It really helps to have friends at many different levels since I have concerns at many different levels as well.

This morning I woke up way too early and wasn't sleepy anymore. I tried to stay in bed for a while but gave up after a while and just got up, puttered around for a little bit and then went to the YMCA for my daily workout. Today I was listening to a book about a fictitious lawyer and the twists and turns in his life. As the story goes today, his girlfriend is shot and ends up in the ICU in a coma. The doctors and nurses are trying to stimulate her into reacting by poking and pinching and speaking to her. In this story she squeezes her boyfriend's hand and eventually wakes up. I'm all of a sudden back in Myrtle Beach trying to get the slightest reaction from Carol. Unlike the story, Carol never reacts and never wakes up. It was all I could do to keep working out without breaking down. No one around me noticed me and I mostly kept my emotions in check, but the similarities between the story and real life were just too great. I know these kinds of things are going to pop up when I least expect them for a long time, but I thought I was safe at the Y. I guess nowhere is safe from my emotions and memories. But it's easier each day.

Bill

Day 64 Journal entry by Bill Funnemark — 12/22/2016

I was trying to run some updates on my phone last night and this morning and discovered a message I had missed from a former colleague sending me greetings and giving me the names a few songs that might offer comfort. The songs were very nice but didn't do much to give me comfort. Instead that just made me miss Carol and bring to my attention how Christmas will be different this year. It's alright Kristi, you were very kind to send the songs. We all have lost loved ones and I guess it's good to remember them, especially at Christmas time.

The other thing Kristi said was that she had tried to send a message several times, trying to get the words just perfect to offer me comfort. There are no perfect words, just words from your heart. I'm no better than anyone else when it comes to having the right words to say. What could I say to my own children and grandchildren that would help fix the hurt? I couldn't offer much. All I could do was hug them and cry. One thing Carol taught me through her death was that you don't have to have perfect or magic words. You just have to reach out to someone who is hurting. I would like to tell all of you who sent me a sympathy card that I read every word printed on the card, but that just isn't true. I did read the first few, but there were just too many. What I did read though was every, single hand-written word. Those didn't rhyme or flow like those of a professional card writer, but they were from the heart. I had to smile at cards with words crossed out or words inserted above because the writer messed up. That's how my cards usually end up.

This morning a lady from Hospice of the Heartland called me to ask how I was doing. I mostly told the truth, but I'm maybe not quite as chipper as I made it sound. I took my Kum & Go cappuccino home to listen to Christmas songs and feel sorry for myself and I was doing a pretty good job of it. But then I was reminded by a couple posts on Facebook that other people have problems too. One young mother, one of my students, has a child who has been in the hospital. That's always scary. One of my teacher friends went to the ER last night with at this point undiagnosed pain in his back. A friend of mine just lost his mother after she suffered another stroke. I guess I'm not the only person in the world who is having a tough time right now and I can sort of understand why the whole world doesn't just stop what they are doing because I just lost my best friend. Suck it up Bill (Mr. F). OK I will, but first I'm going to listen to a couple more songs, shed a few tears and think about Carol. There's no time limit on grieving and I guess I can do it my own way. After all, I've never been accused of following the crowd.

I am so lucky to have so many great friends who care about me and my family. I texted one of these dear friends, she lost her husband not so long ago, this morning to get her help with some of my feelings. I didn't expect an answer right was since it was very early in the morning, but she surprised me with a quick response. I guess she's not totally healed yet either. Thanks SN. The next couple days are going to be very sad at times, but it's just one of those Firsts I have to go through and with help from some really special people I will see it through to the new year. Thank you all and Merry Christmas.

Bill

Day 66 Journal entry by Bill Funnemark — 12/24/2016

I'm sitting in the line to get into Jolly Holiday Lights with the Clapper family. We went to Christmas Eve church, to dinner at Outback Steakhouse and waiting for the lights. This is a Clapper family tradition that Carol and I were fortunate enough to be a part of the last few years. Sitting in church singing Christmas carols was a little hard. Carol couldn't really sing but she really enjoyed listening. It just made me think of past times when we were all together. I actually thought it would be harder on me than it was. I guess I'm getting used to it to some extent.

The line is starting to move. I'm not sure if we will actually get into the light show yet, but at least we're moving. Merry Christmas to all.

The light show was nice with some really cool displays once we got our turn to start driving through. Then it was back home so the kids could go to bed. I have been putting off working on thank you notes because it just looked like too daunting of a task, but I decided tonight would be a good night to work on them. I'm not sure if I followed all the rules of etiquette or not, but I did my best. I will apologize right now to anyone who should be getting a thank you and didn't. I haven't mailed them yet but will on Monday and I'm pretty sure I got 95% of them correct. For those of you who sent me a gift of any kind and you don't get a thank you, I'm sorry. Thank you. That should cover it.

I should be sleeping now but instead I'm updating my journal and waiting for Santa to show up. The only thing I want for Christmas, Santa can't bring. No one can. But I am still very blessed to have three wonderful kids who each have wonderful families. I have other family members who will continue to be part of my life too. And then there are all the friends who God has put into my life over the years. So many of you have reached out to me these past several weeks, some whom I haven't seen in years, others I see on a regular basis. But Christmas is best spent with family and I am so blessed to be able to be with family these last few days and I will be with more family in a few days. I have made the trip to Texas several times by myself, usually on my motorcycle, but I think this will be the first time on four wheels. Carol hasn't always been there. Last year I rode down to be part of Andrew's veteran's day program and Carol stayed home and worked. But this will be my first Christmas at the Hamells without her, just like today is the first Clapper Christmas without her. Another of those Firsts.

I guess I'd best get to sleep now.

Bill

Day 69 Journal entry by Bill Funnemark — 12/27/2016

It's a couple days after Christmas and I'm past one major hurdle. I spent Christmas morning at Mickolyn's home. I expected it to be sad, but no tears were shed while we opened presents. We had a good time, and everything seemed so normal except Carol wasn't there. After we finished opening presents and eating some breakfast, I went down to my room to be alone for a little bit. It struck me that the past couple hours just seemed so normal. It was like no one even missed Carol. We just opened presents and laughed and just a had a good time. I wanted to speak up and say "Hey everyone, how can you just totally ignore Mom/Grandma? Don't you remember she's not here this year?" I held up very well up until this point, but then all the feelings came rushing to the front. I don't mean anything negative about my family, we were all just trying to get through the day and were trying to put a brave face on.

The grandkids deserved a good Christmas. After all, they have been through a very tough time too. It is so easy to feel that I am the only one who is sad, but we all are grieving, each in our own way. For many days through this whole marathon and post-marathon, I have often felt like I'm all alone. My life is in shambles but everyone else just goes on about their daily routine. "Hey world my wife is in a coma. Don't you care? Hey world, my wife just died. Don't you care? Hey world, my best friend is not with me anymore and you just go on about your own business. Don't you care?" That's sort of the way I felt Christmas morning. But in reality, there are so many people who care. We are all hurting. My hurt and pain is different than anyone else's because I was the husband. My relationship was different than everyone else in the world, including my children, grandchildren, in-laws, siblings and everyone else. But that doesn't mean you don't grieve or feel pain. Yours is just different than mine. After I spent some alone time, I came back upstairs and Mickolyn and I worked on thank you cards. I don't know what was said that got us going, but it wasn't long, and we were both sitting there in tears. We had a good cry together, talked about Carol/Mom, shared a few memories and pulled it together and continued working on cards. And life was back to normal, whatever normal is.

Yesterday I stopped by a friend's home for what I thought would be an hour or two but turned into more like six hours. What a great time I had with these friends just talking about our lives and of course Carol. We shared thoughts and memories, cried and laughed, and finally it was just time to go. I have had some sessions like this with other friends too, maybe not this long, but just as intense. I don't know how my friends feel or if they benefit or if they are just being nice and not throwing me out. But I know it sure helps me. It is easier to come home and be by myself, but there are so many reminders of our life together. It gets a little better each day but thank goodness for my family and friends.

Bill

Day 73 Journal entry by Bill Funnemark — 12/31/2016

I wasn't planning on writing anything today because I didn't think I would have any earthshaking comments to make, and I probably still don't. But after reading a couple posts on Facebook, I just felt like writing again. I was reminded how Carol and I had made plans to really enjoy our retirements and we had really just gotten started. We had taken a few trips, a couple of which we even traveled together. One of the things that made our marriage unique is the way we traveled. Carol knew I loved riding my motorcycle, but she couldn't ride with me very far anymore. It bothered her sciatic nerve which gave her pain in her hip. Plus, she didn't think she could spend the extra time away from her consulting job. Even though she was technically retired, she loved going to various nursing homes and consulting. I don't really know what she did while consulting, but she loved it and was very good at it. Carol would encourage me to ride my bike to our destination and she would fly there a few days later. It worked for us. Today being New Year's Eve just brings back too many memories of past trips taken together, separately, and ones planned for the future. We were supposed to go to southern Florida in late February for several weeks. I still plan to go, but it sure won't be the same.

I have talked to a few friends who have lost a spouse and they have shared some of their experiences and how they have coped. One told of how she would dream of her husband sometimes. I haven't had any dreams about Carol until last night. It was a very short dream and she was only in the dream for a brief moment, but it was so real. We, like a lot of people, enjoyed people watching. We'd sit on the beach or at a restaurant and just watch the interesting folks walking by. In my dream last night, we were sitting in some bleachers at some outdoor event, not sure what kind, and a very attractive, older lady walked by who was showing more of her bosom than she maybe had intended. I turned to get Carol's reaction and got a poke in the ribs for my trouble and then a smile and a kiss. Then the dream was over. Just one of those moments from our past. One that probably happened in real life, but that will never happen again. I don't know what 2017 holds for me. The song "I Know Who Holds Tomorrow" by Ira F. Stanphill is one of my favorite songs and one that I sang a few times in church, was sung at Carol's funeral. It's a thought I hold on to each day.

Good bye 2016, bring on 2017.

Bill

Day 74 The End and The New Beginning Journal entry by Bill Funnemark — 01/01/2017

2016 is history and I now move onto 2017. We're all hoping for a better year to come. But as someone pointed out today, 2016 was a pretty good year until the last couple months. Carol and I spent a good part of January in Florida, a week in Miami's South Beach and then some time in Orlando. In March I ran the Myrtle Beach Marathon and then we spent a week at the Ocean 22 resort (the same resort where we were in October) and had a wonderful time. We got to watch some of our grandkids play sports in both Texas and Iowa. At the end of March, I had the honor of being a long-term substitute science teacher for Baxter Community School where three of my grandchildren attended. I got to know a whole new group of kids and parents. Carol and I got to watch Will Clapper compete in several track meets and make it to State Track in the shot put. I finally got to watch Courtney Clapper compete in a couple golf meets and Carol and I were there for her high school graduation. Carol and I found time to take trips to Texas and Oregon as well as shorter trips in and around Iowa. We even had time to sneak in a trip to Branson, MO with Carol's two sisters and her brother -in-law. I even had time to put 24,000 miles on my Triumph.

Carol and I have always known we have a great family. Like all families we're not perfect, but for the most part we all get along. We have a great group of friends, some fairly recent acquaintances while others have been friends for many years. Up until October 20th I really didn't know how many friends we had nor how great our family is. But when Carol suffered a hemorrhagic stroke (a brain bleed) I learned very quickly just how amazing our friends and family are. There have been so many acts of kindness towards me and my family that I can't ever thank all of you or repay you. As tragic as Carol's ordeal and subsequent death were, she was a witness for Jesus through it all. Had she died the first day of her stroke, which the doctors and nurses expected, she would have never touched the hundreds or thousands of people she did. Some of you have praised me for my journal writing and I do appreciate your kind words. But I was and still am writing this for myself. Even if no one ever read a single word, it has helped me get through a terrible time. Somehow God has put words in my head and allowed me to speak to you as an extension of Carol's faith and her life.

This has not been my plan at all. Carol and I had much different plans for our lives and they didn't include her dying this fall. But God had a different plan and he wanted to use Carol to minister to so many people in a way she couldn't do while she was alive. I will probably never know if anyone came to know Jesus as their personal savior through Carol's last days and her death, but I truly believe she did reach someone. 2016 will always be a turning point in my life. Losing your wife, best friend and lover will do that for you. But I also learned so much and came to appreciate people in a way I never have before. And I learned from so many what a wonderful woman and nurse Carol was. I gained a whole new appreciation for critical care nurses and doctors and how difficult their jobs are. I learned how a hospice nurse can be so kind and compassionate to both her patient and the family. I learned how a pastor whom you really don't know all that well can come and stay with you, eat your ice cream and brownies, and become such a special friend in just a couple days. (Actually, Pastor Peter bought the ice cream, so it really was his.)

I will miss Carol for years to come. I know it will get easier as time passes, but I also know the hurt and emptiness will never fully go away. As I move into 2017 I will still talk to anyone who will listen about how I am feeling and my experiences with Carol. But I know your lives for the most part have already moved on to the next big thing. My pain won't be so acute anymore and I will go for days without shedding a tear. But out of nowhere something will trigger a memory and I will break down in tears. Don't feel badly for me or try to avoid me and don't feel like you can't ask me how I'm doing. Don't be afraid to ask me about Carol or what happened to her. I will not be offended. In fact, it is helpful to me to talk about it. Don't be afraid to be my friend. I've been in your shoes, not knowing how to act or what to say, but at least for me I welcome your friendship however you show it.

This seems like a good time to wrap up my journal. It's gone longer than I ever intended it to last, but I think it is about time to stop. I plan to put all my journal entries into one document sometime in the next few months. I have hired an editor to help me with the process. Hired probably isn't the right term, since I don't plan to pay her anything, well at least not much. but between the two of us I hope to have all this in an easy to read format. I don't plan to have a book signing or go on tour promoting my journal. I have no plans of becoming a writer. But when the editing process is completed, I will be happy to share my story with anyone who would like it. You won't find it in Barnes and Noble but I can send an electronic copy to you. Details to follow.

Thank you to all my followers, those who made comments, those who hit the Heart button and those who just read but never commented. I hope you found my words helpful. They were helpful to me if for no one else.

Thank you, God, for all the good from 2016 and the promises for 2017 and use me for good. To Stephanie, Mickolyn and Chad, our family has an empty chair now, but your mom taught you well and she loved you so much. I know I cannot fill the gap in your heart, but I promise to do my best.

All my love,
Dad

Day 78 Be Patient Journal entry by Bill Funnemark — 1/5/2017

I know I said I was done writing, but due to popular demand and my own needs, I will continue. One of my friends asked me to continue for a full year. I can't promise that I will write for a year, but I will continue for as long as it benefits me. Hospice of the Heartland, the organization that ministered to Carol and our family, sent me a packet of information last week. In it was a book titled "Healing a Spouse's Grieving Heart". At first, I didn't even open the packet of information because I was too busy sending out thank you cards, getting caught up on my bills and trying to restore some semblance of order to my house. But eventually I did open the packet and took out the book. I didn't bother reading it, because again I didn't have time. I've been at my daughter Stephanie's home for the past several days and finally started reading it. I am seeing confirmation of a lot of my feelings and realizing there is no right or wrong way to mourn the loss of Carol. There is just my way.

One of the therapies the book suggests is to write things down. So here I am again, writing things down. I am frustrated at times by how slowly things progress. I have been working on getting Carol's life insurance claim settled, which to me seemed like a pretty simple thing. I send a copy of the death certificate and you send me the money. I guess it isn't that simple. Be patient. Carol had two unused airline tickets from two different airlines that I'm trying to get a refund for. This seems like it must be a massive undertaking since it still hasn't happened. Be patient. And now I think back to Grand Strand Medical Center and the staff in the NSICU when Carol was first admitted. They all told me that brain injuries are very slow to heal, and it would take a long time for Carol to heal, if she was going to heal. You just need to be patient. I'm trying to be patient.

I don't think I cried once yesterday. I did get a little emotional a couple times, but I'm not sure if any tears were actually shed, at least not enough for anyone to notice. So maybe I'm making progress on the mourning front. This book I'm reading says I will have ups and downs, and this is normal. Just be patient. The book also points out that I am not half a couple. For nearly fifty years Carol and I were a couple. A few of those years while dating and most as a married couple. We were two individuals joined as one. I don't remember from our own wedding because the church was stiflingly hot, and the preacher talked forever, but I think he probably mentioned that two become one. I feel like half a couple though. My partner in so many aspects of my life is gone, and I don't feel whole anymore. Part of me is missing. But I am one. I am a whole being now. I am not part of a couple anymore. I am single. I haven't been single since high school and even then, I was dating one girl or another most of the time. It seems that society expects us to be in pairs, but I am not part of a pair anymore. I'm not sure how I'm supposed to act or feel. This is one of the realities I'm having trouble getting used to. Be patient.

To all my friends and family who have reached out to me, offered support or a kind word or deed, thank you. I'm new at this whole mourning process and I'm doing the best I can. Just be patient with me.

Bill

Day 79 - Hacksaw Ridge Journal entry by Bill Funnemark — 1/6/2017

I've been staying with my oldest daughter Stephanie in Keller, TX the last week or so. Today started out like just another day, except being in Texas when the high is in the low 20's with a few snow flurries, it really freaks people out. Basketball practice was cancelled, businesses were closing early and evening activities did not happen. So, Steph, her two older boys and I went to the movie "Hacksaw Ridge." I figured this would be a fairly safe event emotionally since it is a movie about a WWII medic. The movie was based on a true story and was very graphic. The main character fell in love with a nurse before he went into the army and of course this nurse wore a white uniform with a traditional nurse's hat. When Carol first started her nursing career she wore the same kind of uniform and it brought back memories of a much younger Bill and Carol. Figure 10 is Carol at her graduation from nursing school, June 1970. She was in nursing school when I left for basic training, so there was some common ground here. This guy was destined to the war in the Pacific while I was probably not destined to Vietnam. His time in the service was very violent while mine was spent in Middle Georgia, the state, not the country.

Shortly before I left for basic training Carol and I went to the John Wayne movie "Green Beret". I know this movie was not a very realistic portrayal of war, but the fact that I was leaving in a few days for basic with a lot of unknowns in my future was still an emotional time for the two of us. I don't in any way want to equate my service in the Air Force to the horrors of going to combat, that's just not my point. But basic training is still basic training and leaving the safety of rural Iowa is a little scary for any young man.

Figure 10

This movie tonight just made me think of Carol from back in 1968 and later after she graduated from nursing school. Her graduation picture reminded me so much of the nurse in the movie, not her looks, but the uniform. Right away I'm on the emotional precipice and the least little nudge was going to put me over the edge. Sitting there in the dark theater watching terrific human carnage still brought back sweet memories of Carol. I can't explain it nor was I ready for it. The tears just happened. Maybe my widow friends (you know who you are) understand it or maybe not. Maybe you've experienced the same kinds of moments, but I was just not ready for this kind of reaction to a bloody, brutal war movie. Thinking about a very special time with Carol, before we were married even, was the last thing on my mind. I guess no situation is safe from sweet memories and sad feelings.

Bill

Day 81 - Journal entry by Bill Funnemark — 1/8/2017

I feel a need today to make a confession. While we were in Myrtle Beach, I started my journal on Caring Bridge on the second day Carol was in the hospital and for the most part I wrote my true feelings and an honest appraisal of the situation. A few days into our stay at Grand Strand Medical Center (GSMC), I felt I needed to share a few more details with close family and friends. Details and feelings, I didn't want to share with the world. Details everyone didn't need to know just then. It was sort of like when a woman first discovers she is pregnant, but only shares this happy news with her husband. A few days later she may share the news with family and finally with the rest of the world. That was me.

Each day I kept two journals. The one journal was on Caring Bridge. The second journal was an email to a group I called family. Family included some actual relatives, but also a few friends who I felt deserved to know a few more details. One thing I shared with family was Carol's real prognosis. To my Caring Bridge followers, I tried to portray hope. But to my family group I was portraying a much more pessimistic outcome. I don't remember what day it was, but very early in this whole process, I knew Carol was not going to get better. From what the doctors and nurses told me and through my own observations, it was clear that she was not improving. By the time she was moved from the ICU to the step-down unit, it was very clear to me that she would never have a meaningful life. If she ever came out of her coma, she would have very minimal function. But her neurosurgeon doubted she would ever come out of the coma.

The time to make a move from GSMC to a different facility had come. My decision at that time was to move Carol back to Algona and place her in hospice care. Many of you thought she was coming back to Algona for recovery and that she would get better. No. She was coming back to Algona to die among family and friends. Before we left GSMC, I asked her doctor how long Carol might linger. I thought since she was breathing on her own and her heart was strong, that she could exist in a coma for months or even years. He told me that it would be more like weeks or days. Carol left GSMC at 7:15 A.M on Monday, November 21st and arrived at Algona Good Samaritan Care Center about 22 hours later. She lived for ten more days, dying on December 1st. Many of you who had followed my journal were shocked when you heard that she had died, because you didn't realize that she was in hospice. I am sorry for deceiving you or giving you false hope, but I was just not ready to share that much information with the world. And my world goes on.

Bill

Day 83 Journal entry by Bill Funnemark — 1/10/2017

I spent the last week or so in Keller, TX with my daughter Stephanie and her family. But this morning it was time to move on. I'm on my way to Southern California to visit a high school classmate for a few days and then on to Oregon City, OR to spend some time with Chad and his family. While at Steph's I got to watch a little basketball, spend some time with the family and even find time to eat a little BBQ. In case you've never driven across Texas, it's a long way across. Usually when I travel either in my car or on my bike, I listen to audio books to help pass the time. There were some trips when Carol and I rode together we'd listen to books too. I finished the book I had been listening to for a few days and decided to just listen to music for a while. Listening to music takes less concentration than trying to follow a story line of a book and as a result, I tend to daydream. So, this morning of course many memories of Carol and my time together came to the surface. One particular memory was a time before we started dating. It was just a memory of a swimming outing at Clear Lake with some other friends or church youth group. I'm not sure of the group or the reason, but it was just a fun and happy time. I have no idea what brought this memory to mind, but it did. A few more thoughts came to mind as well and so I decided I'd better start a new book so I wouldn't be daydreaming about past good times. It's hard to drive with tears in your eyes.

Lots of memories, but as time goes on they are easier to deal with. I can remember our life together without becoming emotional a little more often than a week ago. It still hurts and there are empty feelings, but it is getting easier. A lot of thinking time in the next few days.

Bill

Day 85 Sunny California?? Journal entry by Bill Funnemark — 1/13/2017

I've decided that being in Texas and now California is a better idea than being in Iowa in January. I was invited to come visit a high school classmate and his wife who live in San Clemente. I thought this would be a nice warm diversion from Northern Iowa, but it has been raining most of the day and cold. Well maybe 53 degrees at 10:00 PM isn't all that cold. Don and Lana have invited me into their home to offer me a place to help in my healing process for a few days. Don is the choir director for their church and tonight was practice and I was invited. I didn't know the songs we practiced but I did my best. It seemed like a very safe place to be with little chance of any real emotional encounters. Of course, Don had to introduce me as his guest and why I was visiting. After practice was over, another gentleman about my age came up to me and introduced himself and told me he had lost his wife this past summer. Even though the circumstances were very different, we shared many of the same feelings. I told him about my experience with Carol after she died, and I spent several final minutes with her all by myself in her room at Good Sam. I told him how hard this was for me but also so precious. It was comforting to me when he told me that he had experienced the very same feelings with his wife. I was able to relate my story a little with him and he with me. I thought I was passed getting emotional when talking about Carol and her last days, but I was wrong. Talking to this man just brought it all back in full view.

I'm not sure which one of us was helped more by this brief conversation. I think I could have talked to him a lot longer, but it was time for all of us to go home. But I know that for me, it was another step toward healing. I've been able to avoid thinking about Carol and my loss by keeping busy or as I've been driving by listening to books. But by not keeping my guard up, I find all these feelings are right below the surface and it only takes a little scratch to cause them to come gushing out. The sun is supposed to shine tomorrow. Let's hope so.

Bill

Day 87 Journal entry by Bill Funnemark — 1/15/2017

I've been visiting friends in California for a few days. Don is the music director for their church where he plays his trumpet and directs the choir and Lana sings in the choir. The service was really good but what really struck me was the music. Our good friend Dave has played his trumpet in our home church in Algona off and on for many years. I always enjoyed his playing, but Carol always really loved listening to Dave play. This morning my friend Don played along with the choir and it was so beautiful; it just made me think of how much Carol loved Dave's trumpet. On top of the trumpet music, the choir also sang an arrangement of Amazing Grace, which was one of the songs sung at Carol's funeral. I have been doing really well the last few days keeping my emotions in check, but this morning was really difficult. I have met some very nice people here in California and had a few good discussions about losing a spouse, but it seems no place is safe from fond memories and emptiness.

Monday morning, I am planning on saying goodbye to Don and Lana and head toward Chad's home in Oregon. For many years, Carol would fly to Oregon to help celebrate birthdays sometime during the winter. Now that job is mine. I have spent time with both Stephanie's and Mickolyn's families since the funeral, but this will be my first visit to Chad's home. There will be some emotional times there, but it still should be a good visit, assuming I don't get caught in an Oregon winter storm.

Bill

Day 89 Journal entry by Bill Funnemark — 1/17/2017

I know some of you want me to continue writing and I suppose I will. But I don't have a lot to write tonight. I have been taking a leisurely trip from Texas to Southern California to Oregon, partly to visit family and friends, but also to just get away. I'm not saying I'm avoiding going home, although going home doesn't have a lot of appeal for me right now, I'm more just getting away from familiar settings. Carol and I have been to the west coast many times, but it was usually to visit family. We never drove from Southern California to Oregon, so I am discovering some new territory. If you have never driven or even better ridden the Pacific Coast Highway (PCH), it should be on your bucket list. In places, you are right next to the ocean while a few miles down the road you are inland. As I was driving today, I thought several times that I should stop to take pictures so I could share the beauty, but who am I going to share them with? I know I can post them on Facebook, but my friends back in Iowa get tired of seeing beautiful, sunny ocean scenes and the only one I really want to share them with, will never see them. So, I just keep driving and take pictures with my brain. I stopped at some little Mexican restaurant for lunch. And as I pull up I can't help but think that Carol would be taking pictures of this little place, along with me and my lunch and probably the Audi and me out front. The thoughts kind of put a damper on lunch. I ate my tacos by myself and drove on. Just another memory to be filed away.

Bill

Day 91 Journal entry by Bill Funnemark — 1/19/2017

As I was driving today I had some sweet but painful memories come jumping at me for no reason at all. I should have stopped and written down my thoughts right then, but I thought I needed to keep driving so I could make it to Chad's house at reasonable time. Now I don't remember exactly what the memory was. It could have been the pounding surf of the Pacific Ocean in Northern California or the mountains of Oregon or even something in the book I was listening too. Whatever it was I had to quickly think about something else since I was busy driving. A little later Stephanie called me, and she talked about Pete's new job and their weekend in Nashville. In case you didn't know, Pete, our son-in-law, has taken a new job in Nashville, TN and the family will be moving there soon. While Steph and the boys were there last weekend visiting, Pete's new boss invited them to dinner at Bonefish. We ate a couple times at Bonefish in Myrtle Beach while Carol was in the hospital. The remembrance of those occasions hit me. Carol hadn't even been to this restaurant, but the mention of its name brought back memories of being in Myrtle Beach.

I arrived at Chad's house late this afternoon and was greeted by my three beautiful granddaughters. A tradition for Carol whenever she came for a visit, with or without me, was to take the family to a really good, local Italian restaurant called Bugatti's. To keep the tradition going, that's where the six of us went. A great dinner as always, but it just wasn't the same. Chad and his family are in the process of moving to a different house a few blocks away from their old house. There is stuff sitting all over as you can imagine, since both Chad and Laura work full time and are moving a little at a time. In their bedroom were multiple stacks of clean clothes, waiting to be folded and put away. The first thing I thought of when I saw this was, "Where is Carol when you really need her?" Carol was a clothes-folding machine. If Mickolyn's family knew she was coming to stay for a day or two, they would make sure all their dirty clothes were brought to the washing machine, ready for washing, because they knew Grandma would fold them all and even separate them into the appropriate baskets. Just another little thing that reminds me of you Carol. It's good to be in Oregon, but you should be here with us. I miss you so much in so many ways.

Tomorrow is January 20th. Has it really been three months since I lost you? I know you died on December 1st, but I lost you on October 20th just after our lunch with Ed and Becky. I know you hung on for several weeks, but you could not communicate with me. The last words you ever said to me were, "I think I need to go to a hospital, but I'm so dizzy I don't think I can walk." Just moments or seconds after that you slipped into a coma and never came out. I didn't even get to tell you that I loved you. It seems like it was just yesterday that this whole thing started, but it's been a lifetime ago.

As I'm lying in bed about to go to sleep, it came to me what I was thinking about today while I was driving. So, I am adding this addendum to my earlier post. I am listening to a book about a reporter who gets involved in a major news story and all of a sudden, he is a star. While Carol was in the hospital and later right after her funeral, I was almost like a rock star. I was getting emails and Facebook posts from all kinds of people, old friends and classmates, Carol's friends and my kids' friends. And now most of that attention has moved on to other things and I am pretty much back to being just an old, retired teacher. I don't normally crave attention. I don't ride my bike all over the country to impress people, I ride because I like to ride. I didn't go to a zillion high school events because I needed to be noticed, I went because I enjoyed the games and wanted to support my kids, my biological kids and my CWL kids. Besides not having Carol to share my day to day experiences, I know am not a rock star anymore. Everyone goes back to their own lives and deal with their own problems and forget about me. I'm not being critical of anyone. That's just the way we all are. But for me there is just another piece that is missing. Even in my Caring Bridge posts there were at first many comments for each post I made, but now maybe only one or two.

I am adjusting to my new life. The pain isn't quite so acute, but it is still there. I know I have friends and family who still care, but your lives go on too. I don't expect everyone to mourn with me forever. I have come to realize in these last few weeks while I have been traveling, that in a way I might be avoiding going home. My house is empty. It doesn't represent home to me like it used to. By visiting family and friends I can avoid facing some of the realities that I will have to face eventually. I have never been one to follow the normal script. I tend to do things my way and I guess I am grieving in my own way. Whether it be driving all over the western half of the country or messaging back and forth with a dear friend every night about everything under the sun. Day by day, I'm doing it my way. I'm not a rock star, never was and never will be. I am just a shy man trying to get through a tough part of my life the only way I know how.

Bill

Day 93 Journal entry by Bill Funnemark — 1/21/2017

There are a couple traditions when we come to Oregon City to visit Chad and his family. I already mentioned Carol and or I would always go to Bugatti's for dinner, but Carol would always make at least one visit to Burgerville too. If I was there, I would go along. When I got here Thursday afternoon, we all went to Bugatti's. Lainey, the oldest, said to Chad "It will be a little sad going to dinner tonight and the next day when we go to Burgerville, but going to Jimmy O's Pizza wouldn't be sad because Grandma didn't always go there." Tonight, I took the 3 girls for pizza while Chad and Laura went on a date. And Lainey was right, it wasn't sad at all. So now I'm babysitting. Luckily the girls are old enough to take care of themselves.

Last night Chad and I stayed up way to late just talking. I always figured my kids knew all about Carol and my early lives, but Chad had a lot of questions. When did Carol and I first start dating and who else did I date? When did I go into the Air Force? When did I start teaching and working for Funk Seeds? He had a lot of questions and so many of them revolved around Carol and me. As we talked, I remembered back to when we first started dating and how our relationship ebbed and flowed. I will have to admit that most of the down times were my doing. In my defense, though, I was young, didn't really know what I wanted to major in at Iowa State and really wasn't ready to be a student. But always in the back of my mind, and not very far back, was the realization that if I didn't stay in college, I would be drafted. Going to Vietnam was not my idea of a good thing to do, thus the Air Force. Carol was the one who knew what she wanted to do. It was good to tell Chad a little bit of my story, but it also made me realize that there are parts of our story that Carol needs to tell. I can remember a lot, but I can't tell it from her standpoint. I wish we would have taken the time when we had it to tell our kids all about our early years. Well maybe not all about it. There are certain things about courtship and marriage that your kids really don't want to hear. But it's an opportunity that is lost forever. I will do the best I can, but they will only hear my side of the story. Just another little part of our joint life that is gone.

Bill

Day 95 Journal entry by Bill Funnemark — 1/24/2017

I have been doing quite well coping with my new life. I still think of Carol often and there are things I miss about her and our relationship, but I am moving on I guess. Visiting family and being away from our home in Algona has been a good diversion and has helped keep my mind off things. But every so often reality hits me again. Last night was one of those times. It was too late to write in my journal last night and I just didn't feel up to writing. I was a little depressed because the Packers lost, but I didn't think they would be able to stop Atlanta's offense and I really didn't think the Pack would make it to the Super Bowl, even though I wanted them to and I didn't give up until it was obvious they wouldn't win. Later that evening I was reading through my earlier journal entries, correcting grammatical errors and such things, and it just brought back all the memories. I was kind of looking for the day when I realized that Carol was not going to get better. I know I didn't record in this journal an outright statement to that effect, but I knew it in my heart. Maybe some of you picked up on my change in attitude, even though I tried to remain positive until the end, but I'm sure some of my followers did wonder or suspect that Carol was not really getting better.

Reading those entries just brought back the pain of those first few hours and days. The disbelief that this was really happening was right there in front of me again. I know in my head that Carol is gone, but in my heart, I still feel her near me. I want to talk to her. I want to share with her all that has gone on the last three months. I want to tell her about watching Will, Daniel and Andrew play basketball and how much Trice has improved since last year. I want to tell about taking the Funnemark granddaughters to Jimmy O's for pizza. I want to tell her about driving to California and then driving up PCH to Oregon. I want to tell her about the progress the Hamells are making with their move to Nashville. I want to go to the Flipside with her for pizza. I want to ride with the top down in the Audi and stop at some little dive along the California coast for lunch. I want to touch her, hold her and make love to her. None of these are possible ever again and it really hurts. I miss being with you Carol in so many ways.

I think it was yesterday I talked to Stephanie, although she calls about every day, so I'm not sure when the following conversation occurred. Before the kids went back to their respective homes after the funeral, I gave each a piece of Carol's jewelry. Steph got Carol's wedding ring and she had called to tell me that she had taken it into a jeweler to have it resized to fit on whichever finger she is going to wear it on. The jeweler said a couple of the prongs were worn and should be repaired so she wouldn't lose the diamond. It's ironic that she called me about Carol's wedding ring since Chad and I were just talking about it a couple nights ago. Carol and I got engaged in the fall of 1968. I had completed Air Force Basic Training and was attending technical school at Chanute AFB, IL (Rantoul, IL) and because it was Veterans Day weekend and I had Monday off, I was able to come home for a short weekend visit. We went on a date Saturday evening, November 9, 1968 and we got back to her house, I proposed to her and she said yes. I was making about $110 a month, before taxes and there was no way I had money to buy a ring. I figured a ring would just have to wait. But my dad was concerned that I had not given her a ring. So, my parents lent me some money and Monday morning Carol and I stopped at a jewelry store in Britt, IA and bought a ring. It was a small diamond, but even that was more than I could afford. Years later when we could afford to buy a bigger stone Carol said absolutely not, her ring was special, and she never wanted to replace it.

Steph, when you started talking about Mom's ring, I just had to listen, because I couldn't talk. It is just a ring, but it symbolizes 48 years of commitment to each other. Years of much happiness, some sad times, some trials for sure, but many years of love for each other. I have wonderful memories of our time together and will cherish those memories until my dying days. But memories don't keep me warm at night. Memories don't answer back when I want to talk. People ask, "How are you doing?" And I answer "Pretty well. I'm doing ok." But sometimes that just isn't true. Sometimes I just really hurt inside and am lonely beyond belief. Karen, Suzanne, Andy, Ray and many others know what I mean and know how I feel. You've been through it and are still going through it and I'm sure you still have those days. Yes, for the most part I'm ok, but last night I sure wasn't. Today was a much better day. And life goes on.

Bill

Day 96
Journal entry by Bill Funnemark — 1/25/2017

Most of today I listened to a book as I drove from Oregon City, OR to Twin Falls, ID. Listening to books helps the time go by a little faster and takes my mind off everything else except driving. My book finished a couple hours before my destination, so I listened to music on The Message, a Christian station, and as I drove through the wide-open spaces I had time to daydream. Memories of Carol come to the surface quite readily and most are pleasant. But then I started feeling angry that she was taken from me so early. I know I had nearly 50 years with her, but we were just getting into our retirement years. We had a lot of plans and places we wanted to go. We loved to go to the ocean, walk on the beach, eat at funky restaurants and just enjoy being with each other. We did take several trips before retirement, but they were always limited by work schedules. Retirement would allow us to take longer trips. All of that is over. I know I shouldn't question God and I know He is in control, but right now, I'm not very happy with the whole thing. I can't blame anyone; it was no one's fault. The medical staff at Myrtle Beach did everything they could possibly do, but the damage to Carol's brain was just too extensive. It just seems so unfair and there are days that no words can take away the hurt and emptiness.

Bill

Day 100
Journal entry by Bill Funnemark — 1/29/2017

Before I begin, I just want to make it clear to everyone that this journal entry is in no way political. I don't care about your political views tonight. It seems to me that most presidents have an agenda that they would like to fulfill in the first 100 days of their first term in office. This seems to be some magic number for some reason. I cannot begin to tell you which presidents have been successful with their 100-day goals and for my purposes, it doesn't really matter.

Today is day 100 for me since Carol first suffered her hemorrhagic stroke. This seems like a good time to reflect on what has happened to me, my family and my friends since October 20, 2016. Carol and I were on vacation in Myrtle Beach, SC with our friends Ed and Becky. We had all arrived on Saturday the 15th and now Thursday, we were just finishing lunch at a little bar/restaurant on the boardwalk, when Carol started feeling dizzy. This quickly proceeded to vomiting and unconsciousness, an ambulance ride to the ER where it was determined she had suffered a major brain bleed. Her last words to me were, "I think I need to go to the hospital, but I am so dizzy, I don't think I can walk." She spent the next 31 days in Grand Strand Medical Center in Myrtle Beach, most of which was in the NSICU. On November 21st she was transferred from Myrtle Beach to the Algona Good Samaritan Care Center. After an approximately 22-hour ambulance ride she arrived Good Sam, where she lived for 10 more days, dying on December 1st. Carol never regained consciousness.

What have my 100 days been like? What have I learned or accomplished? How has my life changed? What will the next 100 days bring and the rest of my life? I will attempt to address these questions as best I can. I want to remind everyone who reads my journal, that I am primarily writing to myself. If you want to eavesdrop on my thoughts, you are most welcome.

I started this journal at the urging of my children so that I could keep family and friends updated on Carol's progress and not have to answer countless emails each day. I reluctantly said I would give it a try, but not to expect much. I have never been one to keep a diary or journal, but as I started writing I found it to be therapeutic. It gave me something to do while sitting countless hours in the NSICU watching as

Carol made very little progress and eventually started to decline. My first few weeks I was mostly on autopilot. I got up each morning still not believing that Carol was in a life and death struggle. It was really hard to even imagine that she might actually die. She was too healthy to die, and we had too many years to be together to even think about death. But each night when I would come back to our resort and get into my empty bed, the reality of the whole situation began to sink in. I don't remember exactly which day it was, but sometime early on, I realized Carol was never going to be the same, if she even lived. The support from family and friends was phenomenal and I found myself in sort of an artificial existence. I was on this high from grief, fear, love and other emotions I didn't even know I had. But it was also grueling. Here I was, nearly 1400 miles from home, staying in a beautiful resort where Carol and I should have been having fun, and she was in the ICU fighting for her life.

When we arrived at Good Sam, it was like coming home. Carol had worked there for 30 years and now she was a resident. I was back home too amongst friends, family and Carol's former co-workers. I knew Carol had a very short time to live, her doctor at Myrtle Beach said she might live for a few weeks at the most because her brain had been damaged so severely. Yet how can I give up? The last few hours of her life were so difficult, and I will never forget them. I didn't know how I would react when the final moment came. Would it be scary, would it be too difficult to bear, would she suffer? I thought I was ready. I thought that I had already suffered the hardest part, accepting the fact that she was going to die. I knew it would be sad, but I thought I would be able to handle it. I found out that for me at least, the last few hours were not scary. In fact, there were some beautiful, intimate moments that I will remember always. But I also discovered that the moment her nurse shook her head and said, "I'm sorry, she's gone" were the most terrible words I've ever heard. Nothing could have prepared me for the gut-wrenching pain and emptiness I felt at that moment.

I am doing ok these days, most of the time. It is still hard to go to bed by myself knowing that the other side of the bed is empty. I made an extended trip to Texas, California, Oregon and back to Iowa and at this writing I have still not returned to Algona, but I will soon. During those many hours of driving, I longed for my best friend to be there with me. In the evenings when I was alone in a hotel, I longed for Carol to be there with me or for the opportunity to call or video chat with her, but it was not to be.

What have I accomplished in my 100 days? I have begun to heal. From what I have read and heard from other widows and widowers, I will never stop grieving. I will always have that hole in my life that was filled by Carol. But I am learning to live without her. I have been avoiding dealing with some things, like sorting through Carol's things. They aren't going anywhere and I'm not ready to tackle that job. I have taken care of some business items, but still have other things to still deal with. I am starting to look to the future and how my new life will take shape. I have made no plans to move or sell our house or anything drastic like that, but I am thinking about those kinds of issues. I have learned that life is so precious and so fragile. I've learned there are hundreds of people who care about me and want to help me get on with my life, however that new life takes shape. I've learned that there is no better time than today to enjoy your life and your loved ones. Am I bitter that Carol was taken from me so early? In a way I am. I would have rather had another 20 years together, but I know it was not God's plan for us. I have to accept that we had 50 years together as a couple, 46.5 of those years as husband and wife, and that God gave us the opportunity to travel to many places. We had a lot of fun. We enjoyed being together. We didn't wait until we retired to travel and enjoy the good life. We enjoyed the good life our entire marriage. But I was not ready for it to end.

What are my immediate plans? Carol and I had planned on spending

3 weeks in southern Florida towards the end of February and through the encouragement of family and friends, I still plan on going there. I'm just not sure how it will be. Carol and I always went to the beach together. We were able to go for longer and longer times the last few years and now I will be there by myself. I don't know if I will have fun or if I will be miserable. I know I will miss not having Carol with me. One of the many things I loved about Carol was that she supported me whole heartily on my various motorcycle adventures. She encouraged me to buy my first Triumph because I was having issues with my Yamaha. When my first Triumph had a lot of issues, she encouraged me to trade it for a newer one. It seems my first one was a bit of a lemon. Even though she was not physically able to ride much with me anymore, she wanted me to enjoy my passion. So I will continue to ride as much as I can. I will find excuses to ride all over the country. Sometime this year I will train for and run my 24th marathon. But even this will be a new experience, since Carol has been to every one of my previous ones. Who will drive me to and from the start/finish area? Who will be my cheer team? Who will be my support and ever faithful companion?

A year from now I don't know what my life will be like. I know I will still miss Carol. I know my family will still be there for me. I know God will still be there for me. And maybe, just maybe, I will find some good news that has happened from Carol's death. Did her last few days really touch someone? Did my writing help turn someone's life around? I pray that everything I say, write and do can be a positive influence on the world. I am not trying to change the world. I just hope that I can be a witness to God's graciousness and love even in the midst of my grieving. Let the next 100 days be better than the past 100 days.

Bill

Day 105
Journal entry by Bill Funnemark — 2/3/2017

Through the last several weeks there have been some really good days and some really bad ones. Today fell into the good column. A couple days ago I took a check to the Algona Good Samaritan Care Center for what I think is the last of the memorial gifts given in Carol's honor. I don't know the total amount given since some was given directly to Good Sam and I don't have a record for those donations. But I do know the total was bigger than I ever anticipated. No decisions have been made on how the money will be spent, but rest assured, it will go to benefit the residents there. There were also gifts given to help cover some of Carol's medical and related expenses. The funds over and above our expenses were donated to the Iowa Heath Care Association (IHCA) scholarship fund in Carol's name. I am so humbled by the generosity shown to our family through this whole ordeal. Yes, we had a lot of expenses, but through insurance and donations I'm fine. It just didn't seem right to keep the extra money, even though no one would ever know, I would, and it just wasn't right to keep it. Carol would not have wanted to keep it either. So, a big thank you to everyone who helped me and my family.

Carol was involved with IHCA for many years, serving on the board and in other capacities, and I heard her talk about some of these people but never met any. There were also many other people connected to her Good Sam career and her consulting career. Today I had the chance to meet just a few of them. It was nice to put a face with some of these names and to hear what Carol meant to each of them. It made me feel good to hear all these kind words about her and what she meant to them, but it also made me sad to think about her not being here. Working in geriatric nursing was Carol's calling. She was great at it. I've known that for a long time. But to hear these things again makes me sad too, knowing that she had so much to give and was helping so many people and then to have her life end way too soon, at least in my eyes, just hurts. It just doesn't seem fair.

I had lunch today with a very dear friend. She's actually the mother of an even more dear friend. This woman, about my age, lost her husband very suddenly about five years before Carol died. We had a connection before, but since Carol's death, this bond has become so much stronger. The grieving process takes lots of twists and turns and it seems I never know what's coming next. I think I'm doing ok and then I realize I'm a long way from being ok. After five years this lady's pain is still there and jumps out and overtakes her without any forewarning. I am only two months out from Carol's actual death and I have these moments all the time, not constantly, but nearly daily something will trigger an emotional breakdown. It was really comforting to hear from another person who has been where I am and to know it's ok to breakdown when you need to. We were having lunch in a public restaurant and we were so engrossed in each other's stories that I wasn't aware of anyone else around us. If people noticed each of us taking our turns crying, I was not aware of it. Thank you for the time of healing today. It was good. And for those of you wondering, this was not a date!! It was just two long-time friends sharing stories and lunch. Thanks SN.

Tonight, after my grandson's basketball game, I had another brief encounter that gives me hope. Some of you know that last spring in a moment of weakness, I agreed to do a long-term substitute job at Baxter Community School where my Clapper grandchildren attend. One of the secretaries at the school lost her husband due to cancer. Her son is a senior on the CMB basketball team and she was at the game tonight. After the game was over I watched as she visited with friends and she was laughing about something. I have no idea what they were talking about, but it struck me that here is this woman who has every right to be sad, but she is laughing and having a good time. We did visit for a little bit, and what struck me was that she could be happy and laughing even though she is still grieving. I haven't done a lot of laughing in the past 105 days, but I saw from Julie that it is ok to laugh. I don't have to be somber all of the time.

Today I learned a lesson from two different widows. Each had a different message and whether they knew it or not they each helped me in a special way. Saturday will bring another opportunity to enjoy my family and my life. There are so many things that happen each day that I want to share with Carol, but it's just not going to happen. So I need to enjoy life for the two of us, listen to the voices who are trying to help me and thank God each day for the blessing I receive each day. But it sure would be easier with my best friend by my side. I sure miss you Carol.

Day 107
Journal entry by Bill Funnemark — 2/5/2017

It's the little things. Most of the time each day I'm fine. I have moments that are sad and there are happy memories as well, but every so often a little thing will hit me. This morning in church was one of these times. First, Dave played his trumpet as part of the praise team music. He is very good, and Carol always loved to hear him play. But I sort of expected to have a sweet memory when I first saw him on stage. What I didn't expect came later in the service. I was sitting behind Jim and Cindi, a young couple, well at least young compared to me, and they were just sitting there like any other couple might do. Jim put his arm around her and then each whispered something to each other. It was nothing inappropriate and just a simple gesture that probably no one else noticed, except me. It made me long to touch Carol, hold her in a comforting way that most couples do. I wanted to be able to share some little secret with her, just feel her presence next to me, but it couldn't happen. So many things we all take for granted and really miss when they are no longer possible. One of the things I have learned in the last few months, is to appreciate every moment you have with family and friends. Money and things are important, but relationships are what makes life worth living. Love your spouse every moment of every day, even if you don't always feel like it.

I'm hijacking the Caring Bridge for one night.

Journal entry by Stephanie Hamell — 2/11/2017

This has really become my dad's journal and I always read it and think how he describes so many of the things I'm feeling. But sometimes I feel like I am suffocating with sadness. Like the next minute of missing her will be too powerful to stand...not that I'm considering any drastic measures or anything of the sort, I just miss my mom so much I really can't stand it sometimes. I don't know where else to express that but here. It sucks so much that she died. I'm so sad about it and so angry sometimes. I have moments when I go in my closet and just lose it, I just cry and cry and cry...but really for the most part, I'm ok. We're all ok. I hate to admit it, but I get jealous when I see women my age with their moms. I get jealous seeing couples about Mom's and Dad's age thinking it's not fair. But life isn't fair and no one ever promised it would be. There are many people who have things so much worse than I can ever imagine. People who didn't get to spend as many wonderful years with their mom as I did...she was truly the best. I miss her so much that sometimes it's almost like a physical feeling. Nighttime is the worst and the absolute worst is when I go on Facebook and look at all of our wonderful memories together...but it's also the best because it reminds me of how much we shared and how great our times together were. I realize this is a rambling, disjointed mess of a journal entry, but I miss my mom tonight and it feels good to put on paper (or screen as it was) I'd say I'm about 70% happy most of the time and I really can't complain about that. I'm thankful for what God has given

me, for what He's taken from me and for what He's left for me. Good night...I'm done crying for the night and that always feels pretty good.
-Steph

Day 113
Journal entry by Bill Funnemark — 2/11/2017

I wanted to write last night but it just got too late. I am in between 6th grade basketball games right now and this seems like a good time. Yesterday I spent several hours talking with two different friends, each of us consoling the other. The first contact was with a friend from high school. He is a couple years older than I am, but we played sports together, him better than yours truly. He reached out to me a couple months ago since he had lost his wife to cancer about a year ago. Sharing our thoughts and feelings came easily even after not seeing each other face to face for 50 plus years. The common bond of losing your wife is a natural. He even dated Carol for a short time in high school. This was way before I swept her off her feet and she fell in love with me. I learned about his battle and how he is surviving and some of the struggles I can look forward to. Thanks Andy for a great afternoon, even if you did lose your phone in the process.

Then last night, I talked to another dear friend who lost her husband a while back. What I intended to be a brief 10-minute call, lasted much longer. We had a lot to talk about. One thing that bothers both of us a little, is what other people might think of us either being together or talking to each other. I had lunch with this wonderful lady a few days ago and I am sure some people saw us together. If you have a problem with this, get over it. Neither of us are interested in dating, so don't jump to the wrong conclusion. We are both still grieving and find comfort in being together and talking. Some people may think it is inappropriate for me to be with another woman so soon after Carol's death, but we are just friends. If I was doing the same with a male friend, no one would think anything about it.

Those of you who know me well, know that I have never been one to do things normally. Most people would choose to fly across the country, while I think it makes much more sense to ride my Triumph. I am grieving the only way I know how. This is my first time at it and I am doing what feels right to me. I am not doing anything that diminishes the love I have for Carol or showing any disrespect for her.

One reality I have to accept is that I am not married anymore. For the most part I still feel married, but I'm not. I still think about Carol all the time and I look at life's everyday experiences through a filter of being married. But I am not married. I still wear my wedding ring. I still make the bed the way Carol liked it. I still wash clothes like Carol taught me and not like I did before we were married (when all my whites were more like grays). I hope no one misunderstands my writing today, but these are just thoughts that came to mind. I will do things my way and I will reach out to any resource who I think will can help me. If I can help that person too, all the better.

Thank you for the lunch and conversation KP. We both needed it and we will do it again. Ok, I done venting for today. Now it's time for more basketball.

Day 115
Journal entry by Bill Funnemark — 2/13/2017

Tonight, I was reminded of another couple life events that Carol missed. Earlier today our grandson Will Clapper had his braces removed, revealing his new smile. Grandma never got to see this handsome young man with his new smile. The last she saw him there was still all manner of wire on his teeth. Grandma also missed the final CMB Raider basketball game. The girls lost their tournament game last Saturday and tonight the boys lost their game too. She would have been so proud of Will and the season he had, but also would have praised the whole team, both girls and boys. Collins-Maxwell/Baxter are ending their sports sharing agreement this year, so every sport ends with the last game ever. Grandma missed watching Trice play in several tournaments too. She missed the Hamell boys playing basketball and baseball. She is missing Lainey's basketball season too. Our family loves sports, whether it be basketball, hockey, football, soccer, track or baseball. Have I missed any? Grandma was a real trooper and tried to make it to as many as she could.

A few nights ago, Will, had a really good game and I wanted to call Carol and tell all about it. But just as quickly as the thought popped into my head, I remembered that I can't. I can't share any of these really special moments with her ever again. Stephanie texted tonight with news that they think they have their house in Texas sold, which will let them seriously start looking for a new house in Tennessee. Great news. I'm sure Steph would have loved to have called Mom to tell her all about it. But she can't.

I have many wonderful friends and a wonderful family. They have been so supportive and helped me as I find my new normal, as I learn to be single again, but as great as you all are, you just don't take the place of my wife. I can't snuggle with you at night in my bed. I can't share all the little moments that a husband and wife share with friends or my children. I have become very close to a few people whom I have known for a long time, but never quite in this context. I have always known them from a husband's viewpoint, not as a single man. I'm just not sure how to act. In a couple days I will be leaving for an extended trip by myself. This will be Bill time. I will meet with some friends for a couple days and later with some family, but most of the time will be just me. Many of my followers have commented how much they appreciate my honesty and how I don't hold back. Carol and I booked a condo for three weeks in Palm Beach, FL way last winter and it's already paid for. I am still going, but by myself. I am a little nervous about it because although Carol and I have traveled separately before, we would usually meet at a destination. I'm not sure how I will react to being at the beach without her. How will I spend my time? Will I feel awkward meeting other people? If I understand nothing else about myself from this trip, I should learn what it is like being a single guy again. The last time I was a single guy, I was 20 years old.

I am looking forward to learning how to be single again, but I am also apprehensive about it. I also want to be able to take time to discover what I want to do with my life. Is there another career out there for me? Is there some area of public or Christian service I should pursue? Should I come back and be a substitute teacher and bus driver? My whole life has been turned upside down. I am not interested in being married again but I am interested in being with friends, both male and female. Lots of questions, most of which won't be answered anytime soon, but getting away by myself will give me time to ponder these issues. It will give me time to pray about things and try to discern what God would have me do. I don't like having to make all these decisions. My life was pretty well laid out and we had a workable plan for the two of us and now that plan is shot to pieces. God has a plan for me. I just haven't figured it out yet. But sun, sand and a beach should help.

Day 119
Journal entry by Bill Funnemark — 2/17/2017

About a year ago, Carol and I decided to book a stay at a resort at Palm Beach Shores, FL for three weeks, along with stays at a couple other resorts. This was going to be our longest vacation we'd ever taken. After Carol died my kids asked me if I still planned to go to Florida, even though Mom wouldn't be there with me. I thought it would be a little weird to go to a beach resort without her, but they encouraged me to go anyway. We have traveled separately from time to time, but never something quite like this. I decided to go and try to enjoy myself. Walking on the beach or sitting by the pool just won't be the same without her. I don't know how I am going to feel once I get there. Will I feel awkward? Will I feel lonely? Will I be able to enjoy myself?

Our plan was for Carol to fly to Orlando, I would drive our little Audi there to meet her and then we'd drive on to south Florida. Then we'd drive back to Orlando, she would fly back to Iowa so she could go visit more of her nursing homes and I would drive home. Sounded like a good plan for us, but it just didn't work out. Since the roads in Iowa are currently ice free, it only seemed right to ride my motorcycle instead of driving the car. Day 1 of my trip takes me to Joplin, MO. I had hoped to leave Wednesday morning, but due to some complications, I didn't leave until this morning. Instead of several relatively short days in order to get to where I want to be, I will have three 500+ mile days. Most of today was very pleasant riding and I kept my mind occupied by listening to a book. But I took a break from my book and listened to Christian music. Of course, a few songs came on that brought back many memories of my previous life. My friends have been so good to me and visiting with each of them helps me on my journey, but my friends just can't take the place of Carol.

This was supposed to be a wonderful time for the two of us to be together to enjoy the beach and each other. I still get upset, maybe angry isn't the right word to describe my feelings, but it just doesn't seem fair. Riding my motorcycle is my therapy. Some people just don't understand why I would do this, but Carol understood and even though she might think I was crazy, she would have given her blessing. I know you won't be physically with me Babe, but I know you would understand. Life goes on.

Day 122
Journal entry by Bill Funnemark — 2/20/2017

I left home this past Friday for a trip to Florida and arrived at New Smyrna Beach today. I am spending a couple days with Ed and Becky, before heading on further south on my own. This is a trip Carol and I had planned about a year ago. She was flying down and I would drive our Audi convertible. Since I'm by myself and the roads are free of ice and snow, it only seemed right to ride my Triumph motorcycle to Florida instead. I had a beautiful ride but there were and still are very lonely times. Ed and Becky were with Carol and me at lunch in Myrtle Beach when Carol had her stroke. They are an intimate part of this whole saga. But it is hard to see them too. They are a wonderful couple and have been very special friends for so many years but seeing them again is a sad reminder of four months ago. We took a drive on the beach this afternoon and it was hard to be there without Carol. I know it's something I need to face and it's just another of those firsts. This is the first time back at the Atlantic beach since Myrtle Beach.

I got an email from Chad this afternoon with a letter attached to it. The letter was written by him to Carol dated February 1st. I think that's when he started the letter, but I don't know when he actually finished it. It doesn't really matter. I couldn't bring myself to read it at the time, since Ed, Becky and I were out to dinner. As I read Chad's letter, I remained totally in control of my emotions all the way through the first half of the first paragraph. Hearing his raw emotions and the uncertainty of Carol's condition in those first few hours was just so hard. As awful as it was for me to be with Carol at that time, I can't imagine what my children were feeling as I was feeding them bits and pieces of information as I was learning it from the doctors. Chad's letter was so painful for me to read and relive all that's happened. I'm not going to post his letter or say what's in it, but so many of the words he spoke mimic mine exactly.

I've read that I shouldn't make any major decisions for at least a year, so I am trying to keep some sense of normalcy by continuing with my normal routines. But my normal routine is too hard. I have been in my house in Algona for only a few nights since we left on vacation in early October. Being in the house is just too hard at times. It's easy to find reasons to be gone, some very legitimate and some not quite so much. Going to dinner with a friend, going to their house to talk, going to grandkids basketball games or even taking my car to Des Moines for service provides a reason to not be at home. I know at some point I will need to stay at home and start going through stuff, but I'm in no hurry. I would rather spend time with my friends than stay in an empty house. Thank you friends for putting up with me, for listening to me, for sharing a cup of coffee or a lunch with me, for just being there for me.

Enough rambling for now. The next few days might be really good for me or might be really painful for me, or both.

Day 124
Journal entry by Bill Funnemark — 2/22/2017

I began my late winter Florida trip a few days ago, opting to ride my Triumph rather than driving my car. A great ride to New Smyrna Beach, FL to spend a few days with friends. I had a few moments when I teared up, but I was mostly ok. It was wonderful and hard at the same time to be with Ed and Becky. Wonderful because they have been great friends for longer than I can remember. But very hard because they were sitting right across the table from Carol and me when Carol started feeling sick. They were right there with me when Carol sank into a coma and never woke up. They were right there with me, while I sat in a little consultation room at Grand Strand Medical Center. They were right there with me when a doctor came into the room and told me that Carol had suffered a massive brain bleed and that she is in very critical condition. I just couldn't believe what I was hearing. It couldn't be happening. But it was. Figure 11 is Bill, Ed and Becky at New Smyrna Beach and Figure 12 is me leaving New Smyrna Beach.

Figure 11 Bill, Ed and Becky

Figure 12 Bill leaving New Smyrna Beach

Now I'm staying at Summer Bay Resort, near Orlando. Carol and I spent about a week here last spring with Steph's family. We had a great time. The Hamells went to Disney, while Mom and I did our own thing. We've been to the Disney parks enough. But we also had plenty of family time. When I checked into my room it was really hard being here by myself. No kids here and no Carol here. Just me and my dripping wet motorcycle gear. But this is one of those things I just need to process. While I'm trying to write this, I'm in a group text with my three children, messaging a former student and trying to keep my mind on task. I sometimes forget that I'm not the only one grieving. Yes, I was the only one of my circle who just lost his wife, but my kids lost their mom. My grandkids lost their grandma. Two ladies lost their sister. Several of our family lost their aunt and so on. I miss Carol so much and sometimes I just don't know how to cope. But what hurts even more is to hear my three adult children talk about how much they miss their mom and how it's not fair and how there will be so many things Grandma will miss.

As I continue my trip I know I will have some really hard times. But I will also have some good times to myself to reflect on God's goodness. God gave me so many wonderful years with Carol and no one can take those moments away. I'm trying to stay upbeat for myself and my family. I'm the leader after all. I'm supposed to be strong. But sometimes I'm not sure I'm up to the task. I know I couldn't do it without God leading the way and my family and friends right beside me. Don't feel sad for me. I'm doing ok. I just need to deal with things. Cherish every moment God gives you with your family. When Carol and I were first married, we made an agreement to never go to sleep angry at each other and always kiss good night. I can't say we fulfilled this promise 100% of the time, but we did pretty well. I'm not sure I got a good night kiss after the cable TV guy came to the house (my kids know about this, the rest of you don't. Too bad), but we certainly tried to live up to that promise. Don't waste your time being angry with someone you love.

They might not be there in the morning or any morning, ever again. I love you Carol and I miss you. You should be here in Florida with me, but I'm not angry, just lonesome.

Day 125
Journal entry by Bill Funnemark — 2/23/2017

About the time I think I'm doing ok, I get fooled again by this song. It's titled "Tell Your Heart to Beat Again" by Danny Gokey.

My life has been shattered as anyone who has lost someone so close to you knows. I wasn't planning to write anything today, since it's been a pretty mundane day. But a combination of things just really hit me tonight. I've been chatting with KP, a dear friend and one of my Grief Buddies, and that was good. No sad stuff, just kind words to comfort each other. Then my daughter Steph posted a beautiful picture of herself and Carol from a few years ago. Kind comments followed as one would expect. As I'm looking at this picture and reading the comments, especially the one from Liz, this song started playing on my computer. That's all it took to finish me off. My life changed in an instant back in October and I've been trying to pick up the pieces and put things back together ever since. But the pieces won't go back together. All I can do is let that door close and realize that I need to step into my new life.

I shared with my pastor this morning that my head knows I am now a single man, but my heart still feels like a married man. Everything I do, it seems that I am still feeling married. Not that I asked Carol's permission to do everything, far from it. We were quite independent that way, at least on small things. But every choice I made I tried to make sure it would be one she would agree with. I wasn't always successful, but I tried. But I don't have to please Carol anymore. She's not here anymore. I don't mean that I will do anything to disrespect her or her memory, but I have to think in a different frame of mind now. If I don't want to put the toilet seat down, I don't have to. If I want to drink milk straight from the jug, I can and I do. So beware if you come to my house, stay away from the milk.

A door has closed and I am trying to put my life back together and slowly I am. But I will do it my way and Carol would expect me to do it my way. She would be surprised if I followed someone's guidebook to proper grief recovery. She expected me to do things my way and I will. So if I spend a lot of time talking to my Grief Buddies, so be it. If I ride my Triumph to Florida instead of being logical and driving a car or flying, Carol would just smile and say, "Of course you'll ride your Triumph. I would expect nothing less." Babe I'm trying to put my life back together and I'm doing it the only way I know how. Oh I sure miss you though.

Day 129
Journal entry by Bill Funnemark — 2/27/2017

I finished reading a book today that talks list 100 ideas to help a widow/widower in grieving. Some of these ideas are a little far out there for me at least, but others are very practical. I'm not going to follow all 100, but I have been and still am following many of the ideas presented. One was to take a trip by myself so that I can get away from everyone. Do something you really enjoy. I combined these two ideas by taking a motorcycle trip to Florida. Obviously, I'm not alone. There are thousands of people here, but they are all total strangers. It's not often I could safely take a motorcycle trip from northern Iowa to anyplace in early February, but this year it worked out. Riding by myself is my normal way of travel, especially in the last few years, as Carol, for various reasons, didn't ride with me much. It's a great time to be with my thoughts and not have to communicate with any other humans.

Not that I have anything against communicating with other humans, but I do enjoy the solitude.

This morning I took a nice long walk on the beach, by myself of course, and had a lot of time to contemplate life. Carol and I would walk along the beach talking or not, picking up an occasional seashell, but just enjoying being together and being next to the ocean. As I walked this morning, I couldn't help but think about the many times we had done this same thing together and how it never got old. At times, if I let myself think too much, I would tear up. But most of the time, I just reminisced about our good times and what a wonderful marriage we had. It was a great day of healing.

Later a friend posted a link to the sermon her pastor had given this past Sunday. The pastor titled it his Sex Sermon. Well not exactly, but close. He did talk a lot about sex, love and marriage and how they are part of God's plan. It was just another reminder of what our marriage was based on and why it was so good for so long, and I don't just mean good sex, I mean the respect we had for each other in all phases of our life. We shared everything and tried to please each other in all aspects of our marriage. We weren't perfect. No marriage is, but we did truly love each other. It's comforting to know that all three of our children seem to have marriages much like Carol and I did. This whole sermon was really uplifting for me. Well, most of it was. There were some parts that were sad, but it was mostly positive, and this was from a Lutheran, not a Baptist. Sorry Algona First Baptist (Grace Church), you don't have a monopoly on good sermons. Thanks Kinzee for sharing.

So I was feeling pretty good. Then I got a text message from my daughter Mickolyn, that their son Will had been named 2nd team All-Conference and the team's MVP for basketball this season. Not bad for a sophomore. I'm really proud of Will and all my grandchildren and this was happy news. But then I realized that here is another thing Carol will not see. I did her job and posted a proud grandparent message complete with a few pictures. Carol was always the one who did this kind of thing. As I started to get replies to my post, instead of being so happy for Will, I got angry that Carol is not here to see this. I think about all the things she will miss. I know she's in Heaven and I know God has a plan and all that, but right now that doesn't really help dull the pain or remove the empty feelings I have. We were supposed to be able to share these things. I know, move on and all the other standard responses, but it still hurts. And on it goes, another day with another missing part. I guess it gets easier, but sometimes I wonder. Good night.

Day 132
Journal entry by Bill Funnemark — 3/2/2017

The last few years I have been involved in American Motorcyclist Association self-paced tours. I have never been big with organized, group tours, so these were perfect for me. The first one was a quest for BBQ. The idea was to find as many BBQ restaurants as I could throughout the country, take a picture of it, along with my bike and my numbered flag. I did well that year, finishing in the top five in the country and sampling a lot of BBQ. I also visited all the lower 48 states. The past three years I've been involved in a similar quest, but this time it's called Tour of Honor. The idea is to go to designated memorials honoring the military and emergency organizations. Most states have seven designated memorials, but all states are represented. For riding thousands of miles each year, I might win a t-shirt or a small trophy. The TOH is designed to raise funds for three charities as well as to have fun.

Carol was a huge supporter of my motorcycling activities and encouraged me to visit as many sites as possible and combine these tours with our vacation trips. My quest last fall was cut short when she took ill in Myrtle Beach. I had planned on doing the Four Corners and already had Washington and California. Maine and Florida were to follow, but they didn't happen. I wasn't going to participate in 2017 since I had lost my biggest cheerleader and it just wouldn't be the same. I was given some money by a local group to use as a memorial for Carol or wherever I felt a need. I donated these funds to the TOH charities and explained to the organizers why I would not be riding this year. They accepted my donation but signed me up for free anyway. So, I guess I'm going to be riding the 2017 TOH. It doesn't start until April 1st, but in Florida they have sort of an early bird run. I visited a couple sites yesterday, since I'm in Florida and have my bike here. When Carol was cremated, they put most of her ashes in a large urn that was buried at the cemetery in Algona. But they also gave me a small urn with a few of her ashes, which I have with me on the bike. Even though Carol is no longer with me in body, she is always with me in spirit. The small urn of ashes I carry with me is just a reminder that she is traveling with me one way or another.

At the end of a day of riding, I would always share with her where I'd ridden and some of the cool sites I visited. It just won't be the same this year without having my best friend to share my adventures with. Even though she usually didn't ride with me, she was always a part of my travels. I guess she still is.

This evening after I had posted today's entry, I went to dinner. On the menu was conch fritters. Carol said she'd never eat something like that but once she tried them, she was hooked, so I had conch fritters for dinner. This put me in a remembering type mood. When I walked back to my resort to put my leftovers away, I couldn't help but think that had Carol been with me, we wouldn't have leftovers. I then went down to the beach and just sat in one of the beach chairs still there and watched the waves shown in Figure 13. I very seldom swear, but tonight my thoughts were "Damn, Carol is supposed to be with me at this damn beach. Sometimes life just sucks." I just sat there and cried, because she's not here with me at this beach or any other beach, ever again. Some days just really hurt when you least expect it. The sun will come up tomorrow and life will go on.

Figure 13 Evening on the beach.

Day 134
Journal entry by Bill Funnemark — 3/4/2017

Just a short note today. Yesterday I went for a ride on my Triumph, braving the cool temperatures and high winds. It was near 75 when I left and with wind chill, that's probably 72, but it warmed to a more reasonable temperature of near 80 degrees. I suffered through it. Really was a pleasant ride, but on returning to my room, there was no one there to share my ride experience with. I just settled in to watch the Cyclones play some basketball. That didn't have a happy ending either.

This morning I sent an email to Carol's boss for her consulting position. Carol's and Gwen's friendship goes back many years and it was just a couple years ago, after Carol retired from Good Samaritan, that she started working for Gwen. I just wanted to update Gwen on my travels and how I was doing. Just an innocent email with nothing that should have been emotional or sad. Gwen's response really hit hard. Someone had asked her if she had replaced Carol yet. Yes, she had hired a new consultant, but she'd never replace Carol. It really hit me that professionally, Carol was really good at what she did. I don't know exactly what she did, she'd try to tell me, but I never really knew what she did for over 30 years at Good Sam or with LTC. But what I keep hearing from people who knew her professionally, she was really good. I know there are others who will and have taken over Carol's responsibilities, they will never replace her. To hear another professional nurse tell me that, just really put it in perspective. I'm reading Gwen's email while down by the pool, trying to hold it together (people wouldn't understand why this old guy is sobbing on a beautiful Florida day) and then I read the rest of her email. For me personally, I may sometime down the road find another woman to be my companion and share my life with (I'm not looking), there will never be another Carol. There will never be another mother to our children or another grandma to our grandkids, not like Grandma Carol. That part of my existence is gone forever, and I just don't know how life will ever return to a normal, whatever normal is.

Thank you to everyone who has and is still reaching out to me and trying to help me on this journey. But especially today, thank you Gwen.

Day 137
Journal entry by Bill Funnemark — 3/7/2017

One of my greatest joys in life is music. I like many different genres of music, especially the songs and musicians whom I can understand the words. I like music with simple accompaniment like a simple guitar to music with a full symphony behind it. God can speak to me in many ways. I might read a verse or two that really says something or listen to someone speak a particularly poignant message. But most often I hear a message through music. Music can touch my heart in ways no other medium can. Those of you who have been following my journal since the beginning, October 20, 2016, know that I compared Carol's journey towards recovery to running a marathon. Carol finished her own personal marathon on December 1, 2016 as she crossed the ultimate finish line and crossed into Heaven and into the presence of God and music beyond our comprehension.

I have run 23 marathons in my life, many 1/2 marathons and several other distance runs. One thing that many of these distance runs have in common is music along the way. It might be one guy with a saxophone playing the blues or a large group of singers and about anything in between you can imagine. The music at the beginning of a marathon is fun and entertaining, but in the first five or six miles, it's just entertainment. It helps to set the mood and keep things upbeat. The music that really matters to me is the music at mile 17 or so through mile 20. To me at least, this is the hardest part of a marathon called "hitting the wall." Every marathoner hits this wall due to physical and mental exhaustion. It never ceases to amaze me how a simple song or word of encouragement about this time can give me enough of a kick to keep going, to fight through the pain and hopelessness and continue with the race. It's the music in the back of Waterworks Park in Des Moines near mile 17 or 18 that keeps me going.

Carol finished her marathon, but I'm still working on mine. I don't know what mile I'm on. Some days I think I'm just getting started, while other days I feel like I'm heading down the final blocks to the finish line. I don't mean the same finish line that Carol faced, I mean the finish line of my recovery marathon. Wherever I am, I hear certain songs that keep me going. I see it as God speaking through various artists saying, "It's okay Bill, you can mourn your loss. You can cry if you need to. You can be angry if you feel the need. But you also have a lot to offer. You have a life to live." Two songs have hit me today. The first is one I have mentioned before, "Tell Your Heart to Beat Again" by Danny Gokey. The second song just really impressed me this morning. It's "Fight Song" by Rachel Platten. Her words don't exactly fit my life, but her point seems to be that she doesn't care what others think, she going to take her life back. I miss Carol in so many ways, but I can't let this pain and loss consume me or dictate the rest of my life. I'm determined to take my life back and live it to the fullest. Live it the way I want to live it and not let sorrow and pain control me. I'm not sure yet how this will take shape, but I know Carol would want me to continue to do what I want to do, to ride my motorcycle, to visit family, to make new friends and renew old friendships. Carol would also want me to do it my way.

I have never been a fast runner. I'm not anywhere close to the Kenyans when it comes to running marathons. But I always run the race my way. Whether it be slow or really, slow, I do it my way. I may not make an explosion like Rachel Platten speaks of in "Fight Song", but I will keep fighting. I am recovering, getting on with my life, getting used to being single or however else you want to describe the new me and I will continue to do it my way. Please accept me as I am and the way I run my race. Don't judge me because I'm not running the way you think I should be, (I'm not accusing anyone of this. I'm just venting.) accept me for who I am and what I am trying to accomplish. And know that if Carol were here for my marathon, she'd be on the sidelines at mile 17 saying "Looking good, go for it." I'm trying Babe, I'm trying.

Day 141
Journal entry by Bill Funnemark — 3/11/2017

I'm sitting by the pool at my resort, trying to decide what to write this morning. I have had a lot of thoughts going through my head the last several days, some good and some sad. Yesterday, I went for a long walk on the beach, just listening to music and often, a million miles away. There were happy families with kids digging in the sand, young people tossing a Frisbee, pretty girls sunbathing, old people sitting under big umbrellas, but everyone seemed to be having a good time. As I walked along, I wondered if anyone else was mourning the loss of their spouse. Am I the only person on this whole beach who is not celebrating a special occasion or enjoying a long overdue vacation? No one knew that I am not really on vacation. No one seemed to care that I was walking on the beach by myself. They had no way of knowing my best friend was no longer with me and that I'm staying in a beautiful resort by myself.

I've had friends tell me they think I am very brave to come to Florida on a trip that was supposed to be for Carol and me, but that I came alone. I don't feel brave or strong, I'm trying to enjoy myself and trying to get used to the idea of being single and I am enjoying being in the sun, lounging by the pool or on the beach. But in the evenings when I go back to my room, it's just me. I chat with friends via email, text or messenger or sometimes with a phone call and to those of you who have talked to me one way or another, I want you to know how invaluable these chats are for me. Some chats are brief, while others go on for an hour or more. Sometimes they are silly, lighthearted chats while other times, they are very intense and serious. No matter the content or seriousness, they are all important.

I miss home. It's not that I miss Algona, my house doesn't even seem like home anymore. My house is just a place where I pick up some mail and get a different set of clothes, so I can leave again. Friends have asked me if I plan to sell my house and move closer to my children. I don't know. Do I need my big, old house, with four bedrooms and a mountain of stuff? No, I don't need a place that big. But do I want to move? I don't know. I can't contemplate the possibilities yet. It's just too overwhelming to even think about. I know there is no rush to make these kinds of decisions, but at some point, I will, December 2nd, according to some people. (Inside joke) is when I can start making these major decisions. Being away has given me a lot of time for reflection and to be able to think about my future. I have had no revelations. At times my thought process sort of reminds me of a book my friend Jenny used to make her English class read, maybe she still does. The book is "Black Elk Speaks". In the first part of this book, Black Elk seems to have been high on something and his ramblings make no sense, at least they didn't to me. That's the part of the book that I feel like I'm living right now. I hear things or think things, but they seem to be just disjointed thoughts, with no real meaning, no clear-cut direction. Maybe I need some peyote to help. Just kidding everyone. About as close as I will get to that is inhaling a little second-hand cigar smoke from someone around the pool.

Mickolyn arrives late this afternoon and this will change the dynamic of my stay, in a good way. It will be so good to have some family here. It should be fun, but I'm sure we will share some sad times as well. Steph arrives next week for a couple days too. As great as it will be to have them here with me, I know they will be leaving all too soon. I'm just not ready to come back to Iowa yet. I'm doing ok, just going along each day, trying to get used to my new life.

As a footnote, it must be spring break. This morning by the pool the average age has dropped by ~50 years.

I know I posted this entry a couple hours ago, but I just needed to add an update. As I rode the elevator up to the 3rd floor, I was just struck by incredible sadness. I'm lying on my bed sobbing because I just miss my wife so much. Anyone who thinks I'm so strong, should see me right now. I don't feel very strong. I just feel very sad. It will get better, I know, but today, right now, I wonder when.

Day 145
Journal entry by Bill Funnemark — 3/15/2017

A nearly cloudless sky this cool morning in south Florida. As I sit in my bed looking out at an almost, wave less Atlantic Ocean, my two daughters quietly talking in the other room, I can't think how blessed I am. For some reason I don't understand why God chose to call Carol home and leave me here on Earth, but yet I still feel blessed. I miss my wife everyday and so wish we could be sharing this beautiful morning view, but I know that's just never going to happen. So why do I feel so blessed this morning? I still have my family. My two beautiful daughters, Stephanie and Mickolyn, are here with me for a short time and we have been able to cry and laugh together. No, it's not the same as it used to be, Carol should be here too, but the three of us are know she's gone forever and all we have is our wonderful memories. We laughed that we only remember the good things about Mom. The girls used get crosswise with Mom about stupid stuff, but it's funny how you forget all that stuff and only remember the good times.

I have been able to share a lot of my thoughts with my girls and they have shared theirs with me. Even though their visit will be short, it has been wonderful. I continue to wonder what my future will bring and talking with my girls has helped me clarify things, somewhat. I still don't know what my new life is going to be like, but I'm starting to embrace the idea of being single. Besides my family, I have some very special friends, KP and SN especially, who have helped me on my journey. My friends and family have helped me keep things in perspective. There are days when I am ready to jump headlong into a deep relationship and then am brought back to reality. I realize that I'm not ready for a deep relationship yet. I'm just lonely. I have heard or read about too many cases when a man jumps into a serious relationship a few months after the loss of his wife and then later regrets it. I really have not been single for 50 years between dating and marriage, so being single is a new concept for me. I loved Carol. I loved being with her and being able to share all aspects of our lives. But even while we were married, we enjoyed our time apart from each other. Carol would do things with her sisters or fly to see grandkids without me. I would go for long motorcycle rides without her. We were both fine with that because we always knew we would be back together. But there was always that accountability of letting her know where I was or what I was doing. I did things that fit into her schedule as well as mine.

But a new chapter in my life is in front of me and I am looking forward to it. Don't get me wrong, I wish Carol was here, but she's not and never will be again. I can't change that. I am looking forward to being able to just go for a long motorcycle ride without having anyone expecting me home at a certain time. I love going on trips by myself. I have never been one to ride in a group. Maybe I will start, but maybe not. I love the solitude and freedom of a solo ride. But I also like human contact. I am looking forward to going to a movie with one friend one night and going to dinner with someone else another night. I am looking forward to trying new things. I think I would like to go to some professional production at the Des Moines Civic Center with a friend who really appreciates that kind of thing and then go to a middle school football game the next day and have just as much fun. I look forward to having a friend share a Florida beach with me or a hike in the mountains.

I am also keenly aware that my wife just died, and it is too soon for some of this to happen. Those of you who know me well, know that I have never really cared too much about what people think of my actions. I like to do things my way and really don't care what others think, but I am not totally insensitive to others' feelings. I don't want to put any of my friends in uncomfortable positions and I think they feel the same. If I'm with a male friend no one cares, that's ok with the world. But if I am with another woman, people too quickly jump to the conclusion that we are romantically involved, that we are sleeping together. Trust me, I'm not ready for that kind of commitment. So, if a female friend joins me at an ocean resort some day in the future, we will have separate rooms, and everything will be G-rated.

I've probably said enough for one day. Time to go spend time with my daughters.

Day 148
Journal entry by Bill Funnemark — 3/18/2017

My winter vacation continues, now from Orlando, FL. Carol and I had signed up for a 3-night stay at Parc Soleil Hilton Grand Vacation resort sometime last year. This is one of those stays where you pay almost nothing but agree to sit through a sales pitch. We had decided to book this extra little vacation before we headed back to Iowa. We have stayed here several times before, so it's a familiar place. We were not really into going to the Disney parks anymore, but we did enjoy being in Orlando and this resort in particularly. The downside of staying here is that we have been here before and we should be here now. Again, as I walked into the room, it just seemed so empty. This is a place I should be sharing with Carol or at least family. I will watch some NCAA basketball, go to the pool, take some walks, enjoy a good meal or two and then move on to my next destination.

I will be fine, for the most part. I am starting to get used to the single life, but I still feel married. It still doesn't seem real that I am traveling around to nice warm winter resorts without Carol. It doesn't seem real that when I get back to Algona, she won't be there waiting for me. What's waiting for me at home is a house full of stuff and memories. Memories that I cherish and stuff I don't. The thought of having to go through stuff is daunting. I don't know where to start. I must, but not all at once. There are more important things to do, like going to my grandson's track meets, going to the Baxter Bolt's fundraiser, get the oil changed on my Triumph so I can do more riding. Maybe there's a ride to Texas or Nashville in my future, or maybe even Oregon. The house and all its stuff will be there until I'm ready to deal with it. My grandkids are growing and busy with their activities and they will be over before I know it. Carol used to take mini trips to visit grandkids while I was still teaching. I guess that's my job now. Life sure has a way of taking a sharp turn in one direction when you had planned to go the other direction.

Day 150
Journal entry by Bill Funnemark — 3/20/2017

Five months ago today, my life changed forever. It was about 1:15 PM, October 20, 2016, Carol suffered hemorrhagic stroke. Within five minutes of her first symptoms, she was unconscious, never to wake again. Five months is a long time when you are waiting for something good to happen, like when you're 15 and can't wait until you turn 16 so you can get your license or you're getting married and the wedding date seems like it will never arrive. Sometimes five months can fly by. When you are doing something fun, five months is nothing. Or maybe you are so busy with life, work, family, job and everything else, that time just flies by.

For me, five months has been both. Part of me can't believe that it's already been five months since for all practical purposes, I lost Carol forever. The memories of that fateful day are so fresh. What started like so many other days, with me going out for a run and Carol sitting by the pool, looking out at the beach just waiting for my return, was just another day of vacation. Contrary to what our children think or want to imagine, old folks still enjoy making love. After my run Carol and I returned to our room, to our bed for a little relaxation. Little did we know it would be the final time. A little later we had lunch with friends on the boardwalk, just talking about what we were going to the rest of the day. Then the wheels fell off. At times it feels like yesterday. It can't be five months already. No, Carol didn't die until December 1st, but my last conscious communication with her was on that day.

On the other hand, five months can seem like an eternity. I guess you might say I've been on vacation for most of these five months. I have been traveling, Iowa, Texas, California, Oregon, Iowa, Florida and many states in between. I have visited friends and family all along the way. I have spent a lot of time alone. Time of reflection, time of prayer, time of laughter, time of tears and just time in a fog. I talk to friends and family and this is a comfort, but when the conversation is over, and I reach over to the other side of the bed, it's still empty. These past five months just keep dragging on.

Friends have reached out to me in ways I can't imagine. Friends drove to Myrtle Beach to haul my motorcycle back to Iowa. Friends have bought me pizza at Flipside in LuVerne or dinner at Cinco De Mayo in Algona and lots of other places. I was invited to spend a few nights in sunny, southern California. Today I was even invited to come to Tunisia, as in Africa, by a former student. All of this is great, but the days still grind by.

I've hit a few firsts, but many more to come. First trip to the grandkids without Grandma. First trip to the ocean without Carol. And in a couple days, my first trip back to Myrtle Beach without Carol for a reunion with her incredible medical support staff and the friends I made at the Ocean 22 resort. Then it's back to Iowa for the first CMB track meet without Carol and before you know it, Easter will be here, Baxter prom, Drake Relays, Mother's Day and on it goes. Carol missed Will's entire basketball season, as well as Daniel and Andrew's. So much has happened in the past five months, but in an instant I'm right back at Moe Moon's on the boardwalk watching my best friend slip away forever.

I know lots of you still read my posts. You may not comment or even leave a heart and that's fine. I'm still writing for myself. If you want to keep reading, you're more than welcome. There are days when I think I should call it quits and just end my writing career, but then something strikes me, and I just feel a need to write it down. I have one request for my faithful readers. Please consider making a small donation to Caring Bridge to help keep this forum going. Not just for me, but for those who will come after me and want to be able to share their story too.

Leaving Florida in the morning and on to other adventures. I heard this song today around 1:15 PM, about the time five months ago I lost my first mate. It's been a mixed day. The song is "The Voyage" by Donna Taggart

Day 153
Journal entry by Bill Funnemark — 3/23/2017

Bittersweet. That's how describe today. Had the opportunity to visit with a few of the very special staff members who work here at Ocean 22 Hilton Grand Vacation Resort. There is Dave the parking valet guy and Purnell, Patti and Shani from the registration desk. All made me feel so welcome, almost like I am home. They and many others here at Ocean 22, looked after me, my family and guests last fall. I knew coming back here would be emotional, but it just seemed like something I needed to do. Thank you to all the staff here who helped make my life tolerable last fall and have been so gracious to me now. This resort will always have special significance in my life.

For lunch today, I met with Tanya. We hugged, cried, laughed and then did it all over again. When Carol got sick last fall, she was rushed to Grand Strand Medical Center for treatment. When she arrived in the ER, they rushed her in for a CT scan and determined that she had suffered an extensive brain bleed. From there she was sent directly to the NSICU, where the chief neurosurgeon and nurse Tanya were standing by to do what they could for Carol. She received the absolute best possible care, but the damage was just too severe. Tanya is the only staff member from GSMC who I plan to meet with, but she represents a very classy, top notch facility. Tanya and I were able to share a few memories from last fall, get updates on each other's families and talk about today and the future. We also shared a little nurse humor, but that's a different story.

Then it was time for a walk on the beach. It is chilly here, but not cold enough to stop me from going to the beach. Sometimes the solitude of a walk, listening to some beautiful music can do wonders for the soul. Carol and I had walked this same beach several times, picking up a few shells, feeling the surf on our toes and just enjoying God's beauty. Needing a restroom break, I found myself at Moe Moon's. This is the place where Carol and I shared our last lunch and where my life changed forever. I sat inside and had a cup of coffee, looking out at the table where Ed, Becky, Carol and I had shared lunch a mere five months ago. The table was empty today, which seemed so appropriate to me. I watched happy couples, young and old, walk by and just tried to understand what had just happened. It seemed like only yesterday, that we were sitting there having a great time when the wheels fell off. Coffee finished, I walked to the Piggly Wiggly where we had shopped and bought a few essentials, Coke Zero, orange juice, coffee filters and Cheetos.

It is hard to be here, yet it is so good. A piece of me died here, yet it's still a special place. Carol loved this resort and Myrtle Beach. We had hoped to come back many more times, but plans changed. I brought along a small urn with a few of her ashes. I know that they are just ashes and that she is no longer here on Earth. But these few ashes are a token of our love and our life. She has traveled with me in spirit this entire trip and will continue to travel with me as I make other trips across the country. I plan to sprinkle a few of her ashes on the beach she loved, so that symbolically at least, she will always be connected to this place. My journey continues. What course it takes, I have no idea. I know God is with me every mile I travel, and Carol will always be in my memories right along with me too.

Figure 14 is a picture of our last lunch at Moe Moon's taken a few minutes before 1:15 PM, 10/20/2016.

Figure 14 Last Lunch

Day 155
Journal entry by Bill Funnemark — 3/25/2017

I know many of you who follow my journal are also friends on Facebook, so for you, this will be a repeat from last night. But for others, this will be new. Last night I went down to the beach and spread a few of Carol's ashes. Some went into the water to be carried around the world and maybe deposited on some distant beach. In a way I picture her sunning herself on some beach far away, just waiting for me to join her. Figure 15 is the very last Facebook post Carol every made. It was sunrise over the Atlantic Ocean in front of Ocean 22 Hilton Resort in Myrtle Beach, SC. She had gone down to the beach area to read, enjoy her morning Diet Dew, wait for me to return from my morning run and celebrate God's beautiful creation and the beginning of a new day. About four hours later she suffered her stroke.

Figure 15 Carol's last post

Now fast forward a little over five months. I am back here at Myrtle Beach. I sprinkled a few of her ashes along the beach, above the tide line and a few more in the grassy area above the actual beach. Some of Carol may be picked up by the winds and moved along the beach, maybe even get caught up in the waves, but part of her will remain in front of the resort she loved, forever. Whenever I return, I will know a little piece of her will be waiting for me.

The other pictures represent to me that the sun has set on Carol's life, our marriage and our time together here on Earth. But the waves which continue hour after hour, day after day, year after year for as long as the Earth exists, reminds me that she lives for eternity in Heaven. These dark pictures of an empty beach represent my despair, my emptiness and my loneliness. The bright lights of the resort in the background remind me that someday we will meet in an even more beautiful resort, a resort beyond my comprehension called Heaven.

Just a few thoughts as I continue my journey.

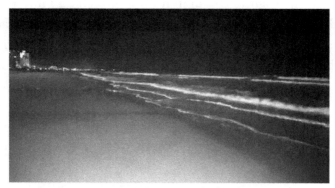

Figure 16 Waves on the beach

Figure 17 Bright lights of Ocean 22

Figure 18 Alone on the beach

Figure 19 A place for some ashes

Day 160
Journal entry by Bill Funnemark — 3/30/2017

I got back to my home in Algona this afternoon after being gone for about six weeks. I wasn't sure this trip was a good idea or not, but my children encouraged me to go. Carol and I had planned this trip over a year ago and I just wasn't sure if it was wise to go without her. It turned out to be a very good trip. Getting away from Algona and all the reminders around our house was good. But unfortunately, they were all still here when I got back. I guess it is time to start tackling some of the tasks that need to be done, like going through Carol's clothes and jewelry, sorting and getting rid of many, many Longaberger baskets and pottery items, disposing of hundreds of paperback romance novels and lots of other stuff. I just don't know where to start. I will get at it, a little bit at a time, but the task is just so unappealing. I think I will go back on vacation.

As I was riding home on my motorcycle this week, I couldn't help but think of Carol at times. She encouraged me to enjoy my passion of motorcycle touring, even though she thought I was a little crazy at times. Maybe I am just a little bit. I was reminded of this a couple nights ago when I stopped near Columbus, IN to spend the night with Carol's niece, Ann, and her family. Somehow, and I won't go into explanations as to how it happened, I have been renamed by her children as Crazy Uncle Bill. I might be just that. But I have always done things my own way. I don't follow a script or live by the book. So, when some people think I was brave or foolish or whatever to take off on my motorcycle, in the middle of February for a six-week trip, I know Carol would have said, "Yes, go for it. Just be careful." She would have prayed for me right before I left the yard, tracked my progress on her cell phone and talk to me every night. She would have worried but have been at peace knowing I was in God's hands. And she would be happy for me, in that I got the chance to do what I love.

Being in love with someone means you want to please them in every way you can. Carol did that for me and I tried my best to always do that for her too. Just another part of my loss is not having her to share the thrill of my ride, or to share what I saw that day, or how nice or crummy the weather was. Now all I can do is share it on Facebook or similar fashion. It just isn't the same. I will continue to ride, and Carol will always be with me. I will visit new sites as well as old, familiar ones and I will share my stories with friends and family. But no one will really care like Carol did. Life goes on.

Day 164
Journal entry by Bill Funnemark — 4/3/2017

This past Saturday marked the four-month anniversary of Carol's death. At 8:13 PM on December 1, 2016, Carol's heart finally quit beating and her life on this Earth were done. I'm still here and I still have things to do and a life to live. I haven't figured out just what this new life will be like, but I'm working on it. I don't mind being alone, being on my own, doing my own thing, but I still enjoy being with friends and family. I remember years ago when my mother died, how Dad gradually was excluded from activities that had previously been a couple's activity. He eventually remarried, partly to fit in with the rest of the world.

When you live most of your life married to one woman, you find that almost everything in your life is for couples. A single guy is the odd man out. Maybe because of what my dad experienced or maybe just my own personality, I like to have a friend who will go with me to do things. I still like going on a solo motorcycle trip, but it is nice to have a friend to share a cup of coffee or to attend a movie with. Saturday night, I was invited to the Baxter Booster Club fundraiser. I donated time at my timeshare in Carol's honor and I wanted to be there to watch it sell, but I didn't want to go alone. I invited a long-time friend who lost her husband a few years ago. We share common ground and I have known her for many years. The booster club event was fun and raised a lot of money and I know Carol would have been very pleased with the event. Thank you SN for a very fun weekend.

I have told my kids that I'm not interested in dating anyone and I have no intention of getting remarried. I am learning how to enjoy being single and how to live as a single man. I want to be able to take off for Texas to visit grandkids if I feel like it, go to a track meet in

Baxter or even take off towards Oregon, just because I feel like it, without having to answer to anyone. But I also love companionship when I'm around, someone who will feed me dinner once in a while, go to a concert, go to a ball game or many other things that non-married couples do. I have a few great friends who unfortunately, have lost their spouse too. It's amazing how this one thing, loss of a spouse, can create a bond with someone. There is nothing sexual or inappropriate about these relationships, but they have developed into very intimate relationships.

Nothing draws two people together like sharing your grief. I find myself talking about Carol a lot, while my counterpart talks about his/her departed loved one. I never understood this until I lost Carol and I doubt anyone else understands it unless they have lost a spouse too. People often have ideas about how widows/widowers should act or how long they should wait to start dating or remarrying. I don't know if there are any rules. I know my kids keep telling me that they just want me to be happy, however that comes to pass. I haven't asked a girl for a date since December 1966 and my situation is so much different now than it was back then. One thing I do know is that I plan to move very slowly. If I was serious about dating, I would take off my wedding ring and stop talking or thinking about Carol in almost every situation. I joked with one of my kids that a wedding ring might be a real turn-off to a potential date and she probably wouldn't want to spend the whole evening listening to me talk about my lover. I still wear my wedding ring and I still talk about Carol a lot. I think it's a sign for me, that I'm not ready to seriously date for a long time to come. If folks have a problem with me having coffee or dinner with one of my special friends, I guess that's their problem. I will continue to do what I've always done, live my life how I want to, in my own way, not how anyone thinks I should live it. Time for bed.

Day 167
Journal entry by Bill Funnemark — 4/6/2017

I am doing great, until I'm not. This week has been a good week. There have been a few times when I was sad, but for the most part things are going great. I feel or felt like I really had things together. Last night though, I found myself in a really horrible frame of mind. One minute my life is going along just fine and I'm enjoying retirement, vacation and all the perks that go along with a healthy, loving marriage. The next minute it's all ripped away. Marriage, at least our marriage, means sharing every aspect of our lives, emotional, intellectual, physical and any other level there might be. All of a sudden this is all gone. Last night, I missed Carol at various levels, I couldn't function like I need to. I was close to making some really bad choices, but I didn't go there. I'm not going into the details; the details don't matter. It was nothing physically destructive. No, I was not contemplating suicide, getting drunk or anything like that. Luckily for me, God put the voice of a friend in my ear and I realized where I was going. I just want my wife back. I miss her so much, that sometimes I just can't think straight. Falling asleep after arguing with God for a while and laying out my fears, my anxieties, my wants and my needs, I was granted a restful night. This morning an angel (not a real one, but sometimes I wonder) happened to call me and I poured out my feelings. Then a workout at the local YMCA and I'm ready to take on the world, maybe.

I made a big step this morning. One of the most intimidating aspects of my new life is go through stuff. I decided to start small. We all have a junk drawer somewhere in our house. We probably have a literal junk drawer as well as a figurative one. The other day I went to our junk drawer to get some batteries. I couldn't get the drawer open because too much junk was crammed into it. There was so much stuff in there, it was hard to find the good things or thoughts all mixed in with the junk or bad thoughts. Time for a cleaning. I did find the batteries, but of course they were dead. Why do I keep dead batteries? There are old spices in there too, all way out of date. The spice that was in my life is out of date, dead, too. I can remember what some of these spices taste like, just like I have fond memories of the spice that Carol brought to my life. But it's time to start finding new spice but being very careful not to go too quickly or recklessly. The first time I tried that hot mustard stuff you get at a Chinese restaurant, I just plunged right in like it was the yellow French's I put on hamburgers. The fire in my mouth about did me in. So are the spices in my life. If I go too far, too quickly, I will get burned.

I am happy to report that the junk drawer is now clean. I don't plan to buy new actual spices, because I wouldn't use them anyway. But I do need other spices in my life. Of course, there are always the standard spices in my life, like riding my Triumph and driving the Audi with the top down, going to family events like track and baseball, but I need some new spices too. A few nights ago, I went to the movie "Beauty and the Beast". This is not on the list of movies I probably would have gone to six months ago. My notion of it before I went, was down there with "Bridges of Madison County". Sorry to all the fans of that movie, but I just couldn't get into a Clint Eastwood movie with no shooting, fighting or male macho stuff. But that's a whole other story. But I actually enjoyed "Beauty and the Beast". I don't have any plans to go to the ballet, but I did try sushi. New spice in my life.

Being single after such a long time of being a couple is hard and I don't know what I'm doing. I didn't know what I was doing when I was 16 and this is one thing age has not improved. I will fumble, make mistakes and go down wrong roads. I will probably make some people mad at me or hurt some feelings along the way. I hope not, but I probably will. God is still working on me. But I now have a clean physical junk drawer. I'm not sure about the one in my head.

Day 169
Journal entry by Bill Funnemark — 4/8/2017

Over the course of the last few months, I've had some really, crummy days, some mediocre days, a few good days and a few really, great days. Today was one those really, great ones. Oh yes, I thought about Carol many times, but they were sweet memories of good times with her on the rear seat of my Triumph. I'm not going to share details, but just know that today was a good day to go for a ride.

Day 174
Journal entry by Bill Funnemark — 4/13/2017

Life moves on. In a few days it will be Easter, another first. Carol won't be here to make ham balls, which was often a staple for dinner. Instead she will be celebrating in Heaven. I wonder if you actually celebrate Easter in Heaven or is it just another day? I will spend the day in Texas with Steph's family.

On my way to Texas a couple days ago, I met with a few friends in the Kansas City area. It was good to see them and visit about Carol and my life and their families. I know during Carol's visitation and funeral, many of her friends spoke to me and said they were Carol's best friend. She had more best friends than any one person deserves. Although some of you were very good friends, there can only be one best and she is Darlene. Very few of my followers ever heard of her let alone met her. But Carol and Darlene grew up together in Wesley. They went to school and Sunday school together. They played sports together and they were there for each other through thick and thin. It's hard to understand how you can have a best friend and not see them for years. Carol and I made many trips through Kansas City, but we never took the time to stop and say hello. Why? Darlene has made many trips to northern Iowa, but never called to have lunch or just talk. Why? I can't speak for Darlene, but for us, we had a schedule to keep. We needed to get to Texas or wherever and just didn't have time. Really, we didn't have time? How lame is that? Now it's too late.

I have done the same thing though. I have been within a few miles of an old friend or one of my students but just didn't take the time to visit. From a practical standpoint it's really dumb, because there is probably free food or a bed for the night if I would just take the time to call. Don't take that wrong friends, just because I call, doesn't mean I'm expecting free room and board. I am joking. We make friends throughout our lives, some for only a few months or years, while others for a lifetime. One thing I've learned from Carol's death is that friends are so important. I hope to tap into this resource from now on. I don't want my friends to come to my funeral and say they hadn't seen or talked to me in ten or fifteen years. Our time is just too precious and our relationships with people are so important.

I have many regrets. I wish I would have saved more money. I wish I would have studied harder in school. I wish I would have been a better husband and father. I wish I would have been a better teacher; actually teaching my subject matter and spending less time telling stories. Really? That's not true. I will never regret spending time with my students, teaching them about life. Science is cool but helping shape a life is so much more important. But I digress. I wish I wouldn't have said certain things to Carol. I wish I wouldn't have sold the little tin box or let the cable guy go upstairs (Inside joke. Don't try to figure it out.) I wish I would have spent more time in prayer with Carol. I wish I would have listened to her more, even when she droned on about proper peri care or many other nursing things I didn't understand. I wish we could have spent ten or 20 more years together. But I can't do anything about all these things. I can do my best with the time I have left, to be a better friend, father and grandfather. I can spend more time visiting people who are special to me, instead of them talking to my children at my funeral about me.

So, I am moving forward. I plan to take more bike trips and I hope to visit people I know all over the country or even around the world. Ten years from now, will I regret that I didn't get through all of Carol's things this summer but instead I visited a friend one last time before he/she died? Ten years from now, will I regret that I didn't keep the lawn manicured perfectly instead of finally riding to see the Grand Canyon? I don't think so. Visit those special people or places while it's still an option. Enjoy life to the fullest while you can. It might not be an option tomorrow.

Day 177
Journal entry by Bill Funnemark — 4/16/2017

I hit another first today. This is the first Easter without Carol, which I spent in Texas with Stephanie's family. Church at 7:00, brunch at Cracker Barrell, to a park to watch Andrew successfully launch his rocket and then back home for dinner with some of Pete's family. Easter service was fine, but every so often, I just couldn't help thinking of Carol. She probably doesn't even know it's Easter. I really don't know about this and have no evidence one way or the other, but I assume when you are in the presence of God, you don't celebrate holidays like Easter and Christmas. But maybe there is a big party in Heaven.

Each first brings me to a time of reflection though. How am I doing in this whole process? Am I doing things the right way, whatever that is? Have I made any bad moves, or have I taken only positive steps? I know I have made mistakes, moved too quickly in some areas and probably too slowly in other areas. I've read the books, listened to some experts, heard stories from other widows/widowers, talked to my pastor and sought advice from friends. With all this, I still mess up and will probably continue to do so. I know there are no hard and fast rules about grieving, but by making certain choices I may help or hinder my overall progress and I may end up hurting people who are dear to me. Sometimes I think I take two or three steps forward and one step back, while other days, I just take a few steps backwards. Unfortunately, I don't always know at the time which direction I'm going. Yesterday I took steps backwards or sideways. Today I went forward though.

When I ask God to show me the way and trust him to help me along that way, I need to be ready to take a turn that I hadn't planned to take. Sometimes these turns can be painful, but I need to trust God to get me to where I need to be. Sometimes the road can be very difficult to follow, and it is easier to take the comfortable route, the route that makes me feel good. But that route may not be the road I should be following. Why don't I just listen to God? Happy Easter everyone. Being with family on another holiday seems to help me get through what could have been an emotional day. Thank God for family.

Day 179
Journal entry by Bill Funnemark — 4/18/2017

Tomorrow morning, I will leave Keller, TX for probably the last time ever. I've said goodbyes to Stephanie's friends and I even said goodbye to the lady at the gas station where I always stop at the end of my run for a French vanilla cappuccino. Of course, they were out of French vanilla today. I'm leaving behind lots of memories and Carol's Jeep. My sixteen-year-old grandson thought it would be a good car for him, so I sold it to him. Carol would be so happy to know that her car is staying in the family. Of course, if she was still alive, she would have probably just given the Jeep to him. Maybe not, but I made him a good deal and it came with half a dozen koozies, some Longaberger fliers and miscellaneous CDs, but no Diet Dew cans.

Carol missed Easter in Texas. She missed news that Pete got a new job that she had been praying for. She missed the news that Stephanie's family would be moving to Franklin, TN. She will miss seeing their new house. She missed out on the opportunity of folding numerous baskets of clothes. She will miss out on some potentially, exciting news about Will Clapper. We'll know more about his news by the end of the week. She will miss out on taking prom pictures of Will and his girlfriend this coming Saturday. She will miss out on so many things that are important to us. Things that help make our lives exciting. But she's not missing out, she's in Heaven. It's us who are left on Earth, who miss sharing these experiences with Carol.

Tomorrow I will board a plane and fly back to Des Moines, hang around the area for the weekend and then come back to Algona. I can hardly wait to get home and tackle another cleaning project. NOT. It will be nice to be home but it's still a full, empty house. Full of stuff, but empty of family. It's just a house. I think I may need a Triumph ride to keep both my bike and me fresh. Even if the weather is bad, I may have to go for a ride or two. I will try to tackle a little bit of cleaning, but it is so hard to get in the mood to go through stuff. Life is good except for all the stuff that sucks. Thanks for friends and family who help me get through each day.

Day 180
Journal entry by Bill Funnemark — 4/19/2017

I have been seeing and communicating with an old friend for the past several weeks, lunch, coffee, a movie, nothing serious. It was good to talk with her about how our lives have changed since losing a spouse. I'm not sure what happened, but this friend sort of hung up on me. I'm not sure what will happen. It is now a few days later and our relationship has been on again off again since I began this entry. I am sure it is off now. I can't explain adequately to KP why we need to back away from each other, but I know for me, it is the right thing to do. This is not what I wanted. I should have known better, but this is my first time at being a widow and I don't know how to avoid all the pitfalls that are out there.

Day 182
Journal entry by Bill Funnemark — 4/21/2017

This morning the official entrants for the high school division of the Drake Relays shot put were published. Of the top 24 shot putters in the state, there is only one sophomore on the list. His name is Will Clapper, my grandson. I'm so proud of him for the success he's had. His hard work is paying off. Not only did he qualify for Drake, this week he was also selected for the National Honor Society at Baxter High School. I should be so excited and upbeat tonight after reflecting on this week. Although I am proud of each of my children and grandchildren for all they have accomplished, it makes me sad. I can't help but think how Carol would have been posting pictures and making loving grandmotherly comments all over Facebook. But she's not. I suppose I should take her place and brag about him, but I just can't get in the mood.

I've had moments of happiness this week from grandkids, spending a little time with friends and family, both in Iowa and Texas, seeing the joy on Connor's face as he embraced taking over ownership of Grandma Carol's Jeep and eating lunch at Andrew's school, to mention a few events. But it has also been a very emotional week for me. I'm excited for Stephanie's family as they make final plans for their move to Nashville, but it is also the closing of a chapter in their lives, a chapter without Carol. She would be so excited to see their new house, to help decorate, to meet the new neighbors, see the kids' new schools. I continue to try to fumble my way through life. I've made some blunders that I wish I could have avoided, but I didn't.

Sometimes when I look to the future, I just get scared of what is going to happen to me. I know I have family and friends who are there for me, but things are just so different. Do I want to stay in Algona or do I want to move closer to family? As some of you have pointed out, it doesn't really matter since I'm never home anyway. Good point. Should I sell my house? What do I do with all the stuff that has accumulated over the past half century? Where would I move to? Do I want a townhouse or a simple apartment? If I move, what happens to my friends in Algona? Will those relationships just fade away? There is just so much to think about, and whenever I do, I come back to the idea that Carol is supposed to be here with me. How can I plan any of this without asking for her ideas?

I don't have very many answers yet and I guess that's ok. The experts say not to make any major decisions for at least a year. I should listen to this advice. Spring is the season of new beginnings, new life. Mickolyn's husband Trent has been busy for several weeks taking care of his new calves, the new life, full of promise. He's been planting corn the past couple days, as a new crop cycle begins. I'm somewhere in the fall or winter of my life, yet it is spring for me, with so many new experiences for me. This life I am living now is almost like starting over. In a way it's like being a 67-year-old teenager. Looking at a new adventure, a new phase in my life, but without a clue how to proceed.

Saturday is about an hour away, another new day and another first. Will is going to his first prom. These darn firsts are getting old and it is still just April. Yesterday was six months since my world collapsed at a beach side table in Myrtle Beach. A moment that changed the lives of so many. A moment that is still as clear as if it just happened. No wonder I'm not thinking straight at times. No wonder my emotions are all over the board. I'm lying in bed, in my bedroom at Mickolyn's house looking at an ocean sunrise picture that Carol took.

In the picture, a new day is just beginning, full of hope and anticipation, and yet there is no hint of the disaster that is looming in just a few hours.

Tomorrow is a new day. God help me to live it to the fullest and in the way you would have me live it. I can't do it on my own, I've figured that much. I need to trust in you. Guide me and open my eyes so I can see the path you have for me to follow.

Day 185
Journal entry by Bill Funnemark — 4/24/2017

Today was a day of two firsts for me. Since Carol died, my life has obviously been altered. Part of the reason I went to Florida this winter was to have some time to think about my future. What I want to do with my life? What do I want to do to occupy my time? I can't spend all my time on the beach. I want to do something that gives back to my community in some form. One of the ideas was to join the Patriot Guard Riders (PGR). This is a group of mostly motorcycle riding veterans who attend funerals for veterans as a show of respect. A few days ago, I decided to take the plunge and join. Some of you may not know that I was in the U.S. Air Force from 1968-1972. I never left the states, never was in any danger, but I still willingly served. As a result, I have always been partial to the military and veterans. If you have been reading my journal for any time at all, you know I like to ride my motorcycle.

My firsts today were twofold. I rode my first mission this morning and I attended my first funeral since Carol died. I rode to Iowa Falls to honor a 93-year-old veteran who served 37 years in the Iowa Air Guard. This was my first mission with the PGR. I then rode to Fort Dodge and participated in my second mission. I didn't know what to expect when I arrived at Iowa Falls and I didn't know what I supposed to do. But the other riders there made me feel right at home. I wanted a way to give back and to be of service and the PGR is a way I can do this. I can go on missions all over the country, but for now I will stay in Iowa. Being part of PGR lets me serve families of veterans and enjoy riding my motorcycle. Today was a good experience and I look forward to doing more missions. The fact that I was at a funeral didn't bother me. I wasn't sure how I would react, but I was ok, most of the time.

Day 192
Journal entry by Bill Funnemark — 5/1/2017

Today marks five months since Carol died. What changes have I seen in my life since that day? Life changed on December 1st when Carol took her last breath, but it really changed October 20th when she slipped into a coma. What has changed and how am I doing? I have done a lot of traveling, seen a lot of my family and friends, shed a lot of tears, accepted numerous hugs, said many prayers and continued to live. I started writing this around 8:13 PM, the time Carol took her last breath. Those last few hours and moments will be forever etched into my brain. As painful as it was, it was still an amazing experience. It's hard to explain. But knowing her struggles here on Earth were over and that she was in the presence of God was comforting and still is. The pain is less each day, but it's still there. Most people who see me think I'm doing great and most of the time I am. Life goes on and Carol would not want me to crawl into a box. She would want me to live a full and productive life. That may be, but I still miss her so much and I'm getting pretty good at hiding my sorrow. Every so often though, I just can't hold it in. Life does go on though.

Day 208
Journal entry by Bill Funnemark — 5/17/2017

It has been two weeks since my last journal entry. What does that mean? Am I forgetting Carol? Am I healing? Am I just tired of writing my thoughts in a journal? Is there nothing to record? The short answers are no, yes, yes, maybe. No, I am not forgetting Carol. I think of her every day. It seems there is always some reminder of her every time I turn around. This past weekend I loaded up a bunch of Longaberger baskets and pottery to be sold. I have a friend who is going to market them for me. He and his wife will do all the work and I just will collect some money. I am parting with a big part of Carol's life as I sell and give away her Longaberger items. She was a dealer for 20 years. The idea was to sell the stuff, but there was more collecting than selling. I've made a start, but I won't run out of Longaberger anytime soon.

I went to a funeral of an old friend today. By old I mean he was 94. All funerals are sad, but I thought it would be safe to attend this gentleman's service. Oh, how wrong I was. As I sat off to the side of my church auditorium but could clearly see the front row. I listened to the message and the music, but the whole time I was focused on the center of the front row, the very seat I was sitting in a few months ago. The feelings all came flooding back. I remembered how it bothered me that the whole church was staring at me, but I felt all alone, even though I was surrounded by family and friends. The gut wrenching feeling of loss and loneliness was just overwhelming. I thought I would be fine, but I quickly realized that I was not ready to go to a friend's funeral. This gentleman had been a Marine in WWII and I thought I should have gone to the cemetery for the graveside service, but I just couldn't go.

I really don't have a lot to say. My life goes on a day at a time. I meet friends for coffee, have lunch with another friend or go for a motorcycle ride with another one. Once in a while, I actually do a little work in my house, but mostly I keep busy going to family events or meeting with friends. It doesn't seem to matter where I go or whom I am with, something always reminds me of Carol. As time goes on the remembrances just become sweeter. But now I'm making new memories, having new experiences, meeting new people and rekindling friendships from a past time. I'm a long way from knowing what direction my life will take in the next few months or years, but I am enjoying myself in this new journey. Even as I enjoy learning what it means to be single again, I still miss the companionship and love of my wife. Friends and family are wonderful, but there is still a huge whole in my heart where Carol used to be. Time is a healer, but I'm a long way from being whole, but I'm getting there, one step at a time.

Day 214
Journal entry by Bill Funnemark — 5/23/2017

Sometimes remembering can be sweet and sometimes it's not. This morning is one of those times. I was listening to a tape of a concert by AJ shortly before she moved away from Algona, but not out of our lives. Carol and I met up with AJ a few times after she moved back to Missouri and a few times when she came back to Algona for a visit. She has many talents, but the one I love most is her singing voice. She sang many special songs at First Baptist Church (Grace Church) but none more special than "It's Christmas Everyday". While listening to this tape of her farewell concert, I couldn't help but think of the wonderful music this lady brought to our church and to times gone by. Some of her songs used pre-recorded background music while others were performed using the best pianist I've ever known, Anita. I was privileged to be able to sing with Ron, Anita, and AJ. I'm not sure how much I added but it sure was fun to sing with them. It brought back some really, good memories of our time together.

Anita went to be with the Lord a few years ago, AJ lives in Missouri, my biggest fan and supporter, Carol, is no longer with us and so it's just Ron and me. Hearing a couple of our songs was so fun to listen to and remember all the good times practicing and singing together. But then AJ sang Carol's favorite song, one of the songs AJ sang at Carol's funeral. The song, "It's Christmas Everyday" was recorded by Kenny Rogers in 1981. It didn't matter what time of year AJ came back to Algona, this song was always Carol's number one request. Hearing this song again for the first time since December 12, 2016 was more than I could handle. I was hit with a flood of emotions, many tears and painful thoughts. As hard as it was, after a few minutes, I was OK. Part of rebuilding my life is going through painful and wonderful memories. Just another day on the way to the rest of my life.

Day 224
Journal entry by Bill Funnemark — 6/2/2017

Yesterday, June 1st, was the six-month anniversary of Carol's death. I tried to stay busy and not think about it, but inevitably those memories came to the surface. But I am better today. I have searched for some meaning in Carol's death, a reason why God would take her from me and her family and friends, but no good answer comes to me. I have searched my heart too for good reasons to continue living myself. Of course, I have family and friends who are there to support and comfort me and I hope that I am a comfort to them as well. It is not just me who lost a loved one, there are so many who also lost a mother, sister, grandma, aunt or friend. Has it really been six months? Sometimes I feel guilty that my life is more or less back to normal. It's a new normal, but I am developing new routines, new friendships and new interests. I still miss Carol so much and I would give anything to have her back, but that isn't going to happen.

I think I mentioned in an earlier post that I have become involved in the Patriot Guard Riders organization. The PGR goes to military funerals and other events to show respect for our service men and women, living and dead. Today I was fortunate to be able to attend a memorial service for an airman who was lost during WWII. Neither his plane nor remains have ever been located, but a service was held in Van Meter, IA at the Iowa Veterans Cemetery today. I have been to only a few of these services so far, but this one was especially touching to me since he was fellow Air Force. The service concluded with a fly over by a KC-135 aircraft. If I do have a new calling, I think it is to attend as many PGR missions as possible. To be able to be a part of this show of respect for our fallen heroes is humbling to me. Each one I've been part of brings tears to my eyes. I doubt that I would be doing this if Carol was still alive. Maybe I would have, maybe not. I just know that this is something I will continue to do.

Day 233
Journal entry by Bill Funnemark — 6/11/2017

I'm back at Myrtle Beach, SC staying at my other home, Ocean 22 Hilton Resort. Carol and I fell in love with Myrtle Beach in June of 2015, the first time we were ever here. I had just retired from my teaching career at CWL and we were off on our first post retirement trip. Often when we traveled, I would ride my Triumph to our destination and Carol would fly there to meet up with me. She was too busy working as a nurse consultant even though she was retired too, to waste time riding to our destination. Our little inside joke. But this time we rode together in our little Audi TT convertible. We didn't stay at the Ocean 22 resort, but a different Hilton resort instead. Ocean 22 wasn't open yet. We met up with our friends Ed and Becky for a fun filled week of sun and fun. Then on the way home we stopped at our friends Mike and Tricia (Pat to me).

Now a little over two years later I'm back in Myrtle Beach, sitting on the 24th floor of my resort looking out at the Atlantic Ocean, just watching the waves. It's a sunny, warm day with a few light clouds and a little breeze. The waves are not large, but they are still there. As I watch them, I can't help but think about the symbolism. Waves are caused by wind blowing across the top of the water. The size of the waves is determined by the strength and direction of the wind and how far away the wind is blowing. A little Earth Science lesson. As a wave moves closer to the shore where it begins to actually look like a wave, you start to see its potential. At first, it's just a little swell, but then it begins to grow and show its real character and potential. But waves don't exist by themselves. They intersect with other waves and in the process their own shape and characteristics change as well as the nearby waves. Sometimes two or three waves collide and cancel each other out. They die before reaching shore and seem to have no impact on the shore. Other waves seem to sneak past and make it all the way to the shore. Occasionally though, two waves converge to form a single big wave and this wave comes crashing into the beach and makes noticeable changes to the beach. And then the water retreats, back into the ocean and is gone forever with only their impact on the beach as evidence of their existence.

Such is life. We all start out as small, insignificant individuals who grow to maturity. Some waves, people, die before they ever reach maturity. Some waves make it almost to the shore but intersect with other waves, people, who cancel them out. They may have been fun to be with 50 yards from shore, but they fade into a distant memory with little to no impact on the world around us. There is the occasional wave, who singularly makes it to shore and makes a lasting impression on society. But these are rare and usually even they have help. But so often two waves collide a way offshore, strengthen each other and come crashing onto the beach. This combined wave moves sand, erases tracks, deposit shells and leave evidence of its existence. And even these waves disappear from our sight, but the really big ones are remembered forever.

The thing about waves is though, it's the same water moving onto the beach. The wave is just the energy that moves the individual water molecules around in different combinations. Carol and I were two waves that intersected somewhere offshore and came crashing into the beach. We were both better by the combining of our energy. I know we each impacted many people as our wave moved onto the shore. But that wave reached the beach and now that wave is gone forever. Just the memory still exists. I'm still out there in the ocean being formed into a new wave. For a while after Carol's death, I saw myself as a lone wave, trying to make it back to shore. But as time has passed, I know there are other waves around me and I will collide with some of these waves. Some of these collisions will be fun, but inconsequential in the long run. There are a few waves that may approach each other way offshore, but it's too early or too far away from shore to know if they will cancel each other out, run side by side but never actually intersect or combine to become one wave. Some waves seem to combine, only to separate again. Waves are fun to watch and are a mystery to me.

I guess I will finish my coffee and then go down and play in the ocean, enjoying the crashing waves.

Day 240
Journal entry by Bill Funnemark — 6/18/2017

Tonight, I'm writing not for me, but for a friend and former colleague, Shannon. I've only known her for a few years, but I've known her family all my life. She taught math at CWL High School for part of the time I taught there too. Today her husband was killed in a motorcycle accident, leaving behind a wife and a young daughter. I'm sure

Shannon had no idea that today would be the last time she'd ever see her husband and father of her child. I'm sure today was going to be a fun Father's Day for the young family. But instead it turned into a day of devastating loss and sorrow. I can't say I know how she feels, because I don't. When Carol died, she didn't leave me with a young child and a whole lifetime to deal with. Our children are grown and have families of their own. But I felt a sudden sense of loss and felt the ensuing loneliness and emptiness, just as Shannon will. Our loved ones died in different circumstances, but the result was the same. I had no opportunity to tell Carol that I loved her. I assume the same is true for Shannon.

The love and support from friends and family really does help in a time like this. As time passes the pain lessens and life takes on its new normal. You deal with the immediate, like funeral details and those kinds of things and then you start to deal with the long-term issues. I have moved on and started my new life just as Shannon will in time, but for now there is a terrible, empty feeling. There is a feeling of loss no one can understand unless they have lost a spouse and even then, Shannon's loss is unique. Sometimes life just sucks.

Day 262
Journal entry by Bill Funnemark — 7/10/2017

I haven't written anything for a couple weeks. I guess I just didn't have anything I wanted to share. But today I do. Forty-seven years ago, July 10, 1970, Carol and I were married on a very hot Friday evening, in the First Baptist Church, which at the time was located across the street from O. B. Laing Middle School. No air conditioning, a very long-winded preacher, two very pregnant bridesmaids and everyone wearing way too many clothes for the conditions. We all survived the ceremony and then proceeded to the basement of the church for lunch and finally our escape to Okoboji for a few short days. A quick trip back to

Wesley, load our car and off we went to Robins AFB, GA, where I was stationed.

Carol had just graduated, top of her class, from Naeve Hospital School of Nursing and now I was taking her away on a new adventure. Like most newlyweds, we had our good times, great times and a few rough patches, but we made it work for 46½ years. This past Saturday I was riding my motorcycle to no particular destination and due to a road closure, I ended up in Albert Lea. I hadn't been in downtown Albert Lea in 40 years and had no idea where I was until I recognized Fountain Street. This is the street where the nursing school and Carol's house was located. Above the door of the old part of the hospital was the inscription "Naeve Hospital". I don't think the house she lived in is still standing, but I knew I was close. Why did God lead me to that street? The image that came to mind was Carol flipping her left hand around in front of her best friend Kathy Jo, hoping she would notice her new diamond ring. It was a very small diamond, but I was barely out of basic training, making maybe a $110 per month. She wore that ring from late fall 1968 until October 20, 2016.

Today I am off the grid, so to speak. I left town early on my motorcycle to spend the day away from everyone and everything. No phone calls, no text messages, no emails, no Facebook posts, just my bike and my memories. As I look back over our time together, I have so many pleasant memories, but also plenty of sad times. The deaths of all four of our parents are especially memorable. In particular, the death of my mom at the age of 49. My dad lived for another 33 years, but I never understood his pain and feeling of loss until I suffered the same thing. I have lost parents, aunts, uncles and friends, but nothing can possibly compare to losing a spouse. Those of you who have lost your spouse understand, especially if you had a good marriage, but the rest of you just can't. I know my family feels the loss at some level, but it is different for them. It still hurts, but just in a different way.

I had a nice ride today, good weather, good roads and good time alone with my thoughts. I recounted many bike trips Carol and I took together, back when she was able to ride with me. We would ride all over the country on bikes not nearly as comfortable as my Triumph and I wouldn't say she never complained, but she was a good sport about it. She didn't even get mad at me when I forgot rain boots for her and we got caught in a cold soaker going through Yellowstone. I did give her some dry socks though. The last few years, motorcycle travel usually saw me riding my bike and Carol flying to our destination. But many of our anniversaries found me working in the corn research nursery for Funk Seeds. Some years, pollinating work was just beginning by July 10th, but many years it was in full swing. For the very few of you who ever worked hand pollinating corn, you know what I'm talking about. For the other 99% of the world, I don't have time to explain it other than to say, "It's not detasseling. A trained monkey can detassel. It takes skill to hand pollinate." Even though I may have spent long hours in a hot corn field, we always had time to celebrate at least a little on our anniversary.

Today as I rode, I thought about the many great times we had during our time together. I remembered vacations with our children, weddings of our children, births of grandkids, graduations and all those events that made us a family. But of course, the painful memories are there too. I remembered our shared grief when someone close to us died, like parents or a special aunt or friend, but mostly the memory of October 20th and the days that followed. Today is some sort of milestone, I guess. I thought I would have a harder time today than I did. I had a few moments when the tears flowed, but for the most part, I just had a day of sweet memories. Another of the many firsts has come and gone and with each new first, life gets a little easier. But it still sucks.

Day 269
Journal entry by Bill Funnemark — 7/17/2017

I think I mentioned a while ago that I had gotten involved with the Patriot Guard Riders group. This is a group of people, mostly veterans, mostly motorcycle riders and mostly men, who primarily attend funerals of veterans in order to show respect and honor our fallen heroes, both young and old. Most of our time at a funeral is spent standing in a flag line, so there is plenty of time to think. Today as I was holding my flag at the cemetery, I started thinking about my own funeral. I am not trying to sound depressing or make anyone feel uncomfortable and I am not planning on my own funeral to be anytime soon, so just chill everyone. But I was thinking about it. Will the PGR be there rendering honors for me? Will it be a really hot day like today? Will the American Legion give me a 21-gun salute? As I attend these military funerals, I am always moved by the ceremony, the presentation of the flag to the family and of course the playing of "Taps." I learned that most of the bugle players aren't really playing though, but instead have a recording in a fake bugle. Kerianne, if you read this, you're off the hook. You've been replaced by a recording.

Another thing that struck me today was a comment someone made to me. We were talking about losing friends and loved ones and recovering from our loss. This person thinks part of the reason I seem to be recovering well is that Carol and I had a really, good marriage and very few regrets. I guess that's true. First, yes, we did have a long, happy marriage and secondly, I have very few regrets, other than the obvious one, that she is not alive any longer. Throughout our marriage, we always tried to put each other first. Sorry children and grandchildren, but you were not the most important part of my life, Carol was. And she would have said the same thing. We went on vacations without our kids. We went on dates without our kids. And when our children left home to make their own families, Carol and I just kept on being in love and putting each other first. Very early in our marriage, we decided to live for now and not wait until retirement to go have fun. I have known too many people who have all these plans for retirement and have saved lots of money, so they can do all these things, only to have one of the partners die or have serious health issues and never get to enjoy each other like you did when you were first dating. I have many fond memories of Carol and our time together, but I also still have a life to live. I wish I had more money, but do I regret taking our last trip? Of course not. There are lots of things on my bucket list, see the Grand Canyon, ride a motorcycle in Alaska (that will give me all 50 states), ride/drive as much of Route 66 as possible, watch my grandchildren graduate and maybe get married someday. That one can wait for a while though. I want to be there when Mickolyn gets her doctorate degree. I want to run at least one marathon a year until I'm 80 or maybe even 90. I want to ride my motorcycle well into my 90s or at least 80s.

Do I miss Carol? Of course, I do. Am I going to stop living just because Carol can't live it with me. No. So in a couple days I will take off on my Triumph and head to Oregon to visit Chad and family. Live your lives now. Don't wait for retirement, because retirement may never arrive. Or when it does, you may find yourself without your best friend to enjoy it with.

Day 273
Journal entry by Bill Funnemark — 7/21/2017

Unless you just started following my journal today, you should already know that one of my passions is riding my motorcycle. As a young boy and young man, I always had a dream of having a motorcycle and riding off on far away adventures. As a boy these adventures were limited to riding around our farm on a beat-up old Cushman scooter. If I were really feeling adventurous, I might even ride it on our gravel road. But since it wasn't licensed and had no lights, off farm trips were rare, usually limited to when my parents were away. As I grew older, I dreamt of owning a real motorcycle, but Mom and Dad were not keen on that idea. So, practicality won out.

Then came graduate school and there was my opportunity. Carol and I were living in Algona and I was working for Funk Seeds as an assistant corn breeder. I convinced my boss to let me try grad school at Iowa State on a part-time basis if I could continue to perform all my duties at Funks. At first the company let me use my work vehicle to commute to Ames and back two or three times a week at no cost to me. Then they decided that this was just a bit too generous and asked me to pay my own mileage. I really couldn't argue with this, but it was also going to cost me a lot. This presented the perfect opportunity for me to pitch the idea to Carol that I should buy a motorcycle, since it would be so much cheaper. With a promise to always wear a helmet, she consented, and my life was changed forever. I rode as many days as possible, even through the winter. This was before I ever had heated gear and some days it was bitterly cold, but I survived.

Being a loving father of three adorable children, I wanted to spend some quality father-daughter/son time with them, just one on one. What better way than to take each one on a motorcycle trip. It would be just the two of us, a little tent and my motorcycle. We had some great trips and it was a win-win for me. I got to ride my bike and spend time with each child. And of course, I figured it was only fair to take Carol on trips too. As time passed and my bike ownership improved, Carol and I would take longer trips, eventually to the Seattle area where Stephanie and Pete lived. Since that first West Coast trip, I have ridden my motorcycle to either Washington, Oregon or California almost every summer for nearly twenty years. Most of these trips I went alone. Carol would fly to either Stephanie's or Chad's home and I would arrive about the same time on my bike. We'd spend about a week with our grandkids and then she would fly home and I would come home eventually.

As I was riding today, it struck me that this trip is different. Almost every bike trip I took to the coast, I would meet Carol there. I might be gone three weeks or more, but I always knew she would meet me at both ends of my trip. I love riding through desolate country, with miles and miles of nothing. I love riding by myself, with no schedule, no pre-planned route and only my own needs to think about. Don't get me wrong, I like having a riding partner, but I also love riding solo. But as much as I love riding solo, I also loved knowing that Carol was following my progress online and pretty much knew where I was all the time. I loved being able to share what I'd seen that day or what adventure I'd had. As I rode today, it hit me that she won't be in Oregon when I get there. Maybe it was seeing the mountains or maybe it was the Facebook memory with a picture of Carol, but whatever prompted the thoughts and memories, it hit me. Another part of my life that is different. Lots of great memories and these are just a few. Tomorrow is another new day.

Day 278
Journal entry by Bill Funnemark — 7/26/2017

Today has been a very difficult day for me. I have been in an on again, off again, mostly on again, relationship with a lady since spring. She is my age, a widow for three years, and someone I've known for over 40 years. She is a wonderful, kind, attractive woman. We started just having coffee or lunch but very quickly became more serious. My family was concerned that I was moving too quickly and that I was just reacting to the loss of Carol. I thought I could handle the situation and keep everything in perspective, but I was wrong. Although we got along very well most of the time, there were some trends I should have picked up on, that were not to my liking.

What do I mean? While visiting my daughter in Texas over Easter, KP and I were video chatting. All of a sudden, she dropped her tablet and screamed, "I can't do this." And just that quickly, our relationship was over. It shocked and scared me that she would act like this and I really didn't know what to do. After a few days we reconciled, came to some agreements and our relationship was back on. I should have taken this as a sign that I should not get involved, but I didn't. Over the next several weeks we became much closer and it seemed this was going to be a long-term thing. There were moments when she would become afraid and pull back from me. I didn't know why this was happening. They just came on so quickly and I had no warning. It was usually a result of something I said, but I could never be sure.

I have felt for some time that she cared for me a lot deeper than I did for her. Don't get me wrong, we had a lot of fun together. She loves to ride my motorcycle and I like having her along. But I feel like I'm on pins and needles around her, thinking if I said or did the wrong thing, she would have a very negative reaction. I was tense all the time. Last night while visiting with Chad's family, something upset her and she wanted to talk. She wanted me to go outside so I could call her and iron it out, whatever it was. I told her that I was busy right then, but I would call in a few minutes. A short time later she wondered why I didn't call her. I told her I was busy.

This was it. Riding out here, I had a lot of time to think and I realized I just didn't want to be in this kind of a relationship. I composed a letter stating my reason for calling it quits. Several messages passed back and forth from early this morning to mid-afternoon, but in the end, I said I was done. I tried to give her my reasons, but she really didn't want to hear them. There is no easy way to break up, someone always gets hurt. I didn't want to hurt anyone, but I also was leery of where this relationship was going. It was not what I wanted, and it wasn't going to get any easier by waiting. It's over. We will both heal in time. It's just very unfortunate this had to happen.

Day 283
Journal entry by Bill Funnemark — 7/31/2017

In a few hours it will be eight months since Carol died and nine and a half months since I essentially lost her. Since those two fateful days, October 20, when she had her attack and December 1, when she actually died, a lot has happened in my life, some good and some bad. Where do I start? I guess I will start with the bad and get that out of the way, so I can end on a more positive note.

I lost the love of my life and I don't know how to deal with that. I've tried to replace that loss by traveling and spending time with family and friends. This has helped somewhat, but there is still that huge hole in my life. It's hard to build meaningful relationships in the best of times, but I'm still in love with someone who can't love me back. I've made attempts, but I am so rusty at this whole dating thing, that I don't know what in the heck I'm doing. I thought dating was hard at 16, but it's a whole new ballgame at 67. My children and grandchildren are trying to be supportive, but they are still hurting too. I have a house full of stuff that depresses me every time I look at it or even think about it. What am I to do with all Carol's stuff? I will slowly tackle it, but I don't really want to.

Every summer since Chad and Laura have lived in either the Seattle area or Portland area, Carol and I would take a trip out there to see them. I'm on my way home from this summer's ritual and although it was great to see them, it was depressing at the same time. Carol should have been there. We loved going to the ocean and although the Pacific is a lot colder than the Atlantic, we still liked to go and take the family for a few days.

This time a beach trip for the family just wasn't going to work, but as I left I took a detour to the ocean and sprinkled a few of Carol's ashes on the beach and in the water. Such a surreal moment for me, realizing these ashes are part of the body of my wife, my best friend and my lover. She is still so very real to me, even though I know she's gone.

Now for some positive thoughts. I've had a very good ride. A few days have been very hot in the afternoon, but for the most part the weather has been good. I even avoided some Wyoming downpours this afternoon. My Oregon family is doing well. My three Funnemark granddaughters are growing like crazy, Chad and Laura are doing well in their jobs and it looks like they are all settled in their new house. When I was there in January, they were still moving in.

I had the chance to visit a young man and his wife last night who live in western Wyoming. Keith was in my middle school Sunday School class many years ago. I'm sure it's true with any teacher that you sometimes wonder if you are making any difference. I know from my days at CWL, that I had an impact on a few. Some even learned a little chemistry or biology. But with Keith I didn't know that I had ever said or done anything to make a difference. I guess I did. Many years ago, I spent the night at his house in Utah and he told me that I had done something right. He said it better than that, but that's the gist of it. Last night he talked about it again. What a great visit we had, in a beautiful home, in a beautiful setting with mountains all around. Thanks Keith and Barb.

I have so many things and people to be thankful for. God has blessed me with a great family who care about me deeply. I have some really good friends too. Things aren't always easy, and they don't always go the way we'd like. Life takes many twists and turns, some painful and some joyous, but for us here on Earth, life does go on. I'm just trying to muddle my way through the best I can.

Day 293
Journal entry by Bill Funnemark — 8/10/2017

Summer keeps plugging along and today I find myself at home in Algona. I spent time visiting friends and family, stopping at home to change vehicles and get some clean clothes. Today I decided it was time to do some downsizing or getting rid of some of our stuff. I still have hundreds of Longaberger baskets and pottery items and since I don't really know where to start on that project, it will be left for a later date. But one project I can handle is getting rid of books.

Carol loved to read for relaxation. Her preferred genre was romance novels, Christian, secular or somewhere in between, it didn't matter. Most had a picture of some hunk of a guy with his shirt undone to his belly button on the cover. I can't say what these books were about for sure, because I never actually read any, but I suspect they had a very common theme. I knew she had a lot of books, but until today, I had no idea how many. I didn't count them, but I estimate there were over 500 books that found a new home today. I know it was a small step in cleaning my house, but it was a start.

I felt like I was on a roll, so I cleaned out her files of old forms and correspondence. I think it is safe to discard basket order sheets from 2000! I also discovered several documents from her consulting job with LTC. Since these had confidential information on them, I felt I'd better shed them. My poor little home shredder was not meant to shred paper for an hour straight. Consequently, it would run for about five minutes before it would overheat and stop. Job completed however, and a lot of useless paper, flyers and catalogs are now in the recycle bins.

I'm not sure what my next project will be, but I think it will involve more donations to Exceptional Treasures. Mickolyn is planning to come home this weekend to help go through Carol's clothes and help decide what to get rid of. My biggest fear in this whole process is that I will discard something that is special to someone in my family. I have a dear friend who lost her father several years ago and treasured his electric razor. Unfortunately, no one knew this, and the razor was discarded. I don't want that to happen to any of Carol's things, but I can't keep everything.

I'm doing pretty well most days. I have been busy visiting family and friends and trying to avoid things that remind me of my loss. There are many days I don't think about Carol or if I do, it's just an innocent, casual thought. I joke with my children from time to time about something their mom had done that I'm reminded of as I go through my day. But there are still those moments when it all hits me right upside the head. A couple days ago I was at a Patriot Guard Mission here in Algona. There was a service at the funeral home, followed by a motorcycle escort to the cemetery. As we approached the cemetery, I wondered where the grave would be located. It wasn't right next to Carol's plot but as I stood in the flag line, I was looking right at it. Funerals are sad at best and military ones are especially so for me. When "Taps" is played I always shed a few tears. This day though I couldn't help but think of the last time I'd been to a cemetery service. Most people there had no idea that I was crying or if they did, they probably thought I was having a normal reaction. One friend understood though, and I thank you for your compassion.

Just so many reminders of a life lived and how things used to be. I'm making my way on this new journey a little bit at a time. Some days are easy, and some are hard. But I guess that's true for all of us. God will see me through this journey and he will guide me through the many twists and turns and when I take a wrong turn, He will be there to get me back on track. So, each day I try to follow the right path, but a lot of days that path is really hard to see.

Day 295
Journal entry by Bill Funnemark — 8/12/2017

Sometimes, in fact most times, it's just the little things that really make me miss Carol. This morning I was up fairly early to run an errand for a friend. I got back home and decided to have a second cup of coffee. On this beautiful morning, a little cool, no clouds and no wind, I'm sitting on my little patio just enjoying the morning. The thought hits me how Carol and I would sit here maybe sharing breakfast or me with a cup of coffee and her with a Diet Dew, thinking we should get busy and do something. But instead we'd just sit and visit or make plans to go for a ride.

Just a sweet memory. God is good.

Day 300
Journal entry by Bill Funnemark — 8/17/2017

I didn't really think I had anything to write today or for the last few days, but a memory triggered the urge to write. While I was checking Facebook this morning, I saw a post from a friend for a song by Donna Taggart's "Jealous of the Angels." I try not to listen to sad songs or songs that remind me of Carol and my loss, but sometimes it just feels good to listen and think. I guess this morning is one of those times. I have had many ups and downs the last several months, but generally speaking, I'm doing well. I've had the opportunity to meet with many friends for coffee or dinner or some activity. These all help my life to get back to normal. I've spent time with my grandchildren and children and this time is always so good. Football season starts soon, which means more time with the Clapper boys. Baseball in Tennessee will be starting soon too, along with maybe some fall basketball, and this will mean time with the Hamell sporting events. Sorry Chad, but I probably won't make it to Oregon for fall sports.

Grandchildren are so precious, whether my own or my friend's, they are all so special. I just played a few rounds of bags or corn hole or whatever that game is called, with some young boys. I'm not very good at it, but it was fun to play with them. Yesterday I got to meet the newest grandson of a friend who is only a couple days old. Of course, I went to the wrong hospital in the wrong city and even the wrong state, but it was a good day for a motorcycle ride, so it didn't matter. A beautiful little man. Aside from the downpour on my ride home, it was a good day. One of my grandnephews, age six or so was baptized in a river near his home in Indiana this last weekend. I did not attend, but it is heartwarming to know that he understands enough about Jesus to want to be baptized. To him, I am Crazy Uncle Bill. Where did that ever come from? That's another story for another day. My Oregon family just purchased a new puppy, a 17-pound black lab, who is just adorable. I wish I could be there to meet this new arrival to Chad's family.

As I think about the many blessings I have experienced over the past year, I am so grateful for family and friends. Some of these experiences would have never happened if Carol was still with me, but many others would or could have. I don't understand why she had to die. I know God has a plan for me and I'm trying to find it, but it seems pretty illusive. So, I just go a day at a time and try not to think of what I've lost, but instead of all the blessing I have had. God is still good.

Day 304
Journal entry by Bill Funnemark — 8/21/2017

It is just a few minutes past midnight on August 21, 2017. I spent the weekend at Mickolyn's house spending time with friends and family. I went to bed a couple hours ago but have been listening to music and just messing around on my computer. The whole time I've had this empty feeling. This is nothing new, since I always have an empty feeling, but I couldn't figure out why tonight. I've had a fun weekend and nothing traumatic happened, nothing to make me sad, just a good time.

Then I hit me. Ten months ago, October 20th, was the day Carol was taken from me. She didn't die that day, but she had her brain bleed, lost consciousness and never spoke or acknowledged me again. She did respond to a few people for a few days, but never to me. I tried to get her to respond in the smallest of ways, but the damage was just too great. The memories of those first few hours are so clear to me and I doubt I will ever forget them. A lot of what happened in the next few weeks is sort of a blur, but not those first few hours.

We had just finished lunch with friends, Ed and Becky, at Moe Moon's in Myrtle Beach, SC when Carol complained of a headache and being extremely dizzy. In a very few moments she was vomiting and passed out. EMTs arrived on the scene very quickly and she was rushed to Grand Strand Medical Center in Myrtle Beach. In less than 45 minutes from her first symptoms, she was in the hands of one of the top neurosurgeons in the southeastern US. I texted my children as Ed and Becky drove me to the hospital. I told them that something happened to Mom and she was going the hospital, but I have no idea how serious things were.

When we first arrived at Grand Strand, the ER didn't have a record of Carol being there, but they said to just wait a few minutes and give the ER staff time to get her entered into the computer. I checked back 10 or 15 minutes later, and the desk receptionist made a call and then asked me to go to this little consultation room. This did not seem like a good sign. She gave me no indication of her condition but said that a doctor would come out shortly to talk to me. I remember sitting in this little room all by myself just waiting. I finally peeked and motioned for Ed and Becky to come join me. In what seemed like an eternity, a doctor finally came into the little room and the worst few minutes of my life played out in front of me. He told me that Carol had a massive brain bleed and that she was in extremely critical condition. I thought I would be strong and be able to handle anything, but I lost it. When you hear a doctor tell you that your wife is near death and her prospect are not very good, nothing else matters. It really hit me that Carol would very likely die.

How do I tell my children? What do I tell them? Do I tell them to get to Myrtle Beach as quickly as you can if you want to see your mom before she dies? Will there even be time for them to get here? I don't know how they all three made it, but somehow God provided a way and they were all there by noon on the 21st. I don't know how long they stayed, a few days, a week, I don't know. Those details escape me. I know all four of us were like zombies taking our turns keeping a vigil. Carol amazed the staff by not dying. We were told later that over 90% of people who come in with this severe of a bleed don't survive 24 hours. Carol lived for 43 days. She spent her last few hours on Earth in the very nursing home where she had worked for 30 years.

As painful as those minutes, hours, days and now months were and have been, I am doing well today. I still have many sad moments, but not every day now. I think of Carol often and what we will never do together again, like watching grandchildren play football, baseball, basketball, soccer or any other activity. We won't be sitting in the front of the church when Courtney gets married or at the ceremony when she graduates from college and all the way down to Addy, when she does the same. She won't be there when Will runs through the tunnel onto Jack Trice Field to play in his first college football game. She won't be at my 68th birthday party in a few weeks and she won't be there to cheer me on when I run my 24th marathon sometime this fall.

Those are just a few of the things she will miss. These make me sad, but I have to deal with it. I'm trying to make sense of my new world and sometimes I think I'm doing a good job. But then I turn around and do something dumb. When experts say to go slowly and to not make any big decisions for several months, they know what they are talking about. This coming Saturday will be our 50th high school class reunion. Carol and I graduated form Corwith-Wesley High School as part of the Class of 1967. We were both looking forward to this occasion, reconnecting and reminiscing with old friends. But this Saturday I will be sitting by myself in a crowded room. This might be a really hard evening, or it might be a wonderful evening or maybe both. I miss you Carol.

Day 309
Journal entry by Bill Funnemark — 8/26/2017

Today was Carol's and my 50th high school class reunion. We started dating in December of 1966 during our senior year at Corwith-Wesley High School. We were the Class of 1967 and if my math is correct there were 37 students in our class. I think there were 15 classmates plus spouses and guests in attendance, six who have died, a couple who planned to attend but had some conflict and couldn't be there and the rest just didn't come. I guess that's about right.

How fun it was to see old friends, some I haven't seen for many years, and to be able to recall fond memories from our high school days. I wasn't sure how I would feel seeing my old friends. Would it be awkward? Would they shy away from me not knowing what to say? Would there be a lot of questions about Carol and what had happened? It was not awkward. I think most everyone has been following my journal or at least knew a little bit about Carol's death. But I was given an opportunity to speak to the group and tell them just what had happened and how I'm doing today. I felt right at home with my friends and they all were very kind to me. I wasn't looking for sympathy, but they showed genuine compassion for my struggles.

One of the benefits of a reunion is to find out where everyone is living now. Many of my classmates still live in Iowa, but others live in Colorado, Wisconsin, Florida, Arizona, Minnesota and even Mexico, just to name a few. Renewed friendships mean new invitations to come visit. I think there might be some trips in my future. One of my classmates mentioned that you make friends in college or church or workplace, but if you change jobs or move, these friends soon become just memories. But the friends you made in high school, especially if you went to a small school like CW, last a lifetime.

I'm glad my reunion wasn't in March, because I don't think I would have enjoyed it nearly as much. I'm sure everyone would have been nice to me, but I don't think I would have been ready to hear all the reminders of days gone by. Carol and I were high school sweethearts. And even before we started dating we knew each other for as long as I can remember. Our ties to Corwith-Wesley as students and then many years later to Corwith-Wesley-LuVerne as a teacher were so important to both of us. Our school building is gone, now just a grass field, but those memories live on forever. Thank you, Class of '67 for your caring and compassion for me these past several months. We weren't the best class, nor were we the worst. We were just a bunch of kids who grew up in a very difficult time and now here we are 50 years later, not as much hair and more of it gray, a few artificial joints, a few more aches and pains but a lifetime of experiences. We've all experienced sadness, hard times and good times, but those of us still living have that to be thankful for. We miss those who went before us and our numbers will probably be fewer at the next reunion, but for those who were able to be together tonight, life is good.

Day 315
Journal entry by Bill Funnemark — 9/1/2017

As time passes, I go through ups and downs. It's hard to know when an up is going to hit me and it's equally hard to predict when a down is going to slap me up side the head. I left Iowa a few days ago on my trusty Triumph heading for Gatlinburg, TN for the Labor Day weekend and a birthday celebration with my youngest grandson, Andrew Hamell. I took three days to make a two-day trip, but I was in no hurry. I just enjoyed the ride alone with my thoughts with no pressure to put on a ton of miles to reach my destination. The weather was great, except for some rain this morning. Thankfully, I missed any bad storms that may have been passing through the area. I was looking forward to watching the Baxter Bolts and my grandson Will Clapper play football. The game was going to be carried over a computer feed, so I could watch it this evening. The Bolts are in their first year of eight-man football and it is a new experience for Will and the rest of the Baxter High School supporters. Will, as a lineman, doesn't touch the ball, but in the eight-man game, he is an eligible receiver. He caught his first touchdown pass as a varsity player, but I missed it because the computer feed froze right about then. It was still a big thrill for all of us. But in just a few more plays he left the game with an injured knee. Hopefully it is not serious. One minute I was on a high and the next I'm on the bottom.

These same feelings of ups and downs come in all forms. It might be from a football game or a motorcycle ride. One minute the sun is shining, and it is a gorgeous day for a ride and the next minute you're riding in the rain. One minute I'm feeling happy and content with my life and the next minute I think of Carol and I might fall in a deep hole. A very dear friend sent me a very nice email today with a song title I needed to listen to. I couldn't listen right then since I was in a truck stop and had no wifi to download the song. But when I got to my room in Gatlinburg, I downloaded and listened to "Goodbye" by

Lionel Richie. It was also recorded by Kenny Rogers. I sat and listened to this beautiful song several times with tears streaming down my face. I know many of you have lost friends and family members, but only a few of you have lost a spouse. Those of you who had a good marriage and lost your mate too soon, you will understand how powerful this song is. One of the things that really hit me while listening to this song was that I can't hear Carol's voice anymore. I have lots of pictures of her and I look at them often, but I don't hear her voice. I don't hear her laughing or her crying. I don't hear her when she's frustrated with her computer or with me. I don't hear that sweet voice when I did something nice and she whispers something sweet to me.

I know it's a little thing, but it still hit me hard. We had plans and saying goodbye was not part of them. Carol always told me that she couldn't live without me and because of that, she would go first. Niether of us planned on finding out this soon if one of us could go on without the other. I have some wonderful friends who, along with my family, make this journey bearable. Thanks to all of you. And for the record, goodbyes, especially like Carol's, really suck.

Day 325
Journal entry by Bill Funnemark — 9/11/2017

I just spent several days with my daughter Stephanie and her family and am now on my way back home. Since 2008 and the birth of Andrew, we have spent Labor Day weekend with the Hamells. I don't remember if I was there in 2008, but I know Carol was. This year I was there but Carol wasn't. We celebrated Andrew's birthday with some fun activities and a few baseball and basketball games. I had a fun trip but just like so many of my days, there was a big void, someone missing. Just another one of those first events.

Tomorrow is my 68th birthday. We didn't always spend it together because of our schedules sometimes didn't allow. But we always celebrated, if not on the 12th, then a few days later. We quit giving each other gifts years ago since neither of us needed anything, but I could always plan on a card. Sometimes it would be a sweet, romantic card. The next time it would be a funny or even slightly naughty card. I will miss not getting that card from her tomorrow. This coming weekend I will celebrate my birthday and watching football with family and friends at Mickolyn's home. It will be another bittersweet weekend.

As I work my way through my first year I have gone through many ups and downs. There are days when I feel great. Today while riding I just thoroughly enjoyed myself, no worries, nice day, good roads and nice scenery. I even came to a ferry across the Ohio River, see Figure 20. Now a ferry shouldn't be anything emotional, but it was a reminder of times past. Always in the past when I had the chance to cross a river via ferry, I've always had someone special to share this uncommon experience with. If I lived near Seattle, a ferry crossing would be no big deal, but living in northern Iowa, it is a bit unusual. It's nice to have someone special to share these experiences with. It's these little things that hurt so much. But each day gets easier.

Figure 20 Crossing the Ohio

Day 335

Journal entry by Bill Funnemark — 9/21/2017

A letter to my honey:

Happy birthday Carol. Today you would have turned 69. How did we celebrate your birthday last year? I drove the school bus for Bishop Garrigan and you were in LeMars doing consulting work. The next two days you worked in Des Moines. We went out to dinner on Thursday the 22nd, Friday we went to Will's football game and then on Saturday we went to an Iowa State game. It was a great extended weekend. This year is a whole lot different. There were many years that we didn't celebrate our birthdays on the actual day because one or both of us was busy with work. But we always celebrated. We stopped giving each other birthday gifts many years ago because we had both come to that stage of life when you needed or wanted something, you just went and bought it. But we always exchanged cards. Once in a while you would give me a serious card. I never did. But usually our cards were funny, sometimes a little on the adult humor side. Special things that two old married folks shared with each other and no one else. In 2015 we took a motorcycle ride to Illinois and spent the night at a bed and breakfast somewhere along the Mississippi back on the Iowa side. Most recent years we would celebrate our birthdays with the Clappers, since they are relatively close to Algona. Some years it would be a joint party, while other years we'd each warrant a party.

This year, it was just a party for me. Today I am celebrating your birthday alone. I think I will go for a run when it gets light. Maybe I will go eat some cake. HyVee might have small cakes. Or maybe The Chocolate Season has something that resembles a birthday cake. This afternoon I will drive the bus for the YMCA. This is a pretty tough gig. I have two stops and if I go really slowly, it takes half an hour. Baxter has its first home volleyball game tonight and I thought about going to that. Will's girlfriend is one of the captains and they have a pretty good team. You know how much I love volleyball, but I might go anyway. Will is hoping he gets clearance from Dr. Warme to play football on Friday. Will had the stiches removed on Monday and he thinks he's ready to go, but he needs to get the OK from Dr. Warme and Mom. I plan to just stay at Mickolyn's house this weekend and then go to Trice's game on Monday.

Then it's back to Algona. Wednesday evening Tom and Gail invited me to participate in a car/motorcycle cruise around Algona. I guess several people have done this the last Wednesday of the month all summer as a fund raiser for Shriner Hospital. This time we meet at the Chrome, drive around Algona and then go eat. I haven't decided if I will drive the Audi or ride my Triumph. Do you remember four years ago, you bought me a new 2013 Triumph Trophy for my birthday, sort of? I actually bought it, but we joked that it was my birthday present. Then two years ago at your suggestion, I traded it in on a new 2014 Trophy. It was the same model, same color, same everything, but without all the little glitches the 2013 had and about 47,000 fewer miles on it. Now two years later, I traded again. I think you would approve. It just made sense to trade. My 2014 had about 55,000 miles on it and Jeremy made me an offer I just couldn't refuse on a new 2017, same color, same everything.

Since you no longer need your Jeep, I sold it to Connor last spring. He was thrilled to get it along with your GPS and a couple dozen koozies. I'm not sure why you needed all of them in your Jeep, but we had a good laugh and a tear as we thought about you and your Diet Dew addiction. I hadn't planned to give Connor your GPS, but he asked if he could buy it and I knew that you wouldn't dream of charging him for it, so it was just part of the deal.

On another subject, what were you ever going to do with all of the Longaberger things you had? Everywhere I look, there are baskets and pottery. Yesterday I went to the farm and loaded a dozen or so totes of Longaberger stuff and brought them back to town. I know you loved them, and you enjoyed selling them, but to me they are just things. There are a few that are special to me, like the Super Bowl XLV champions, Green Bay Packers basket, but most are just things. So, I am having a garage sale, sort of like the one you had a few years ago. It will be October 19-21, which is a year after you had your brain bleed that lead to your death. This won't be the happiest memory I've had, but it seems like a good time to have a sale. Erika is letting me use the second floor at The Chocolate Season to display your baskets and Jan is coming to help price stuff. Thank goodness for Jan, because I don't have a clue. I need to go through your things and get rid of stuff I no longer need. I've started on your clothes but haven't made much progress. I did get rid of some of my old clothes though and the hundreds of paperback books you had accumulated. I felt that dealing with the Longaberger items took priority. When I'm done with the garage sale I'm going to Myrtle Beach to spend a few days at Ocean 22, our home away from home. It will just be me this time, but you will be there in my memories. How I cherish our vacation getaway memories as well as all my memories. I don't know if birthdays are special in heaven or not, but I'm sure you are having a wonderful time. Oh, how miss you Carol Jean Leek Funnemark. Why did you have to die so soon? I wasn't ready for you to go. I miss you and I love you.

Day 344
Journal entry by Bill Funnemark — 9/30/2017

On this last day of September, I wasn't going to write anything, but I changed my mind. I am in Franklin, TN for a few days visiting Stephanie's family. Daniel, their middle son, asked me a few weeks ago if I would come down and play golf in a fundraiser for his school's basketball program. There was no good reason why I couldn't. So here

I am. Golf is not my strong suit, but we had fun. I was trying to stay up and watch a movie with Pete, my son-in-law, but I was mostly sleeping and decided to head to bed. Listening to some music before I go to sleep, I'm struck with loneliness or maybe an empty feeling. I spend my time these days visiting family, watching grandkids play football or baseball and visiting friends. But at night, not every night, but often, I am just so lonely. Even though I have family just outside my door, I am all alone.

I know I have said this before, but those of you who have never lost a spouse, just don't understand. My children miss their mother, but they go on with their own lives, as I do. But they still have that intimate partner to complete their life, to comfort them, to share the little things from the day. Once you are married, you don't share that part of your life with your parents or your children. You share them with your mate. I wanted to tell Carol about my golfing day, Connor's chip shot that went in from maybe 30 feet, fantastic drives or not, and just my day. I wanted to tell her all about the exciting win Baxter High School had last night and how Will intercepted a pass. But I can't.

Maybe I miss Carol a little more today because I had a strange dream about her last night. I'm not sure where I was, home maybe, and she came walking in the room. She walked a little unsteady and seemed a little confused, but she was aware her surroundings. As you probably know, I am planning on have a basket sale in a few weeks to get rid of a lot of the Longaberger items I have. I have already gotten rid of a few things. She was upset with me because some of her baskets and pottery were missing and wondered what I'd done with them. I asked her what she was doing here, that she is dead. I watched you die, and I have your ashes. You can't be here. She really couldn't explain that dilemma, but she wasn't too concerned about it. Now I have no idea what this dream means, if anything, but it was weird.

There are so many things I'd like to tell her. I want to hold her tight and make it all better. I want things the way they were. I want to tell her about Courtney's boyfriend, Will's and Connor's girlfriends and maybe even Daniel's if he actually has one. I want to tell about how well all the grandkids are doing in school and sports. I want to tell her how near Mickolyn is to completing her doctorate degree at Drake. I want to justify my purchase of a new motorcycle. I want to tell her about some of the Patriot Guard missions I've gone on and how special they are. I want to tell that I cry for no apparent reason when I hear a song. I want her to fuss over my sore knee and be my own personal nurse. I want her to pray for me when I leave on a trip, whether a short or long one. Family and friends have been so kind by trying to fill some of these functions, but it's just not the same.

As I was listening to music this song "Silver Medals and Sweet Memories" by the Statler Brothers, really hit me. I know it's not exactly the same, but something about it hit me.

Bring on October. Hopefully this one will be better than October 2016.

Day 352
Journal entry by Bill Funnemark — 10/8/2017

This morning as I was getting dressed, I was listening to some Staler Brothers' songs. They play their own style of country and gospel music, some funny, some patriotic, some religious and some that just make me remember. The one that just hit me today is "What We Love to Do." I wasn't a wannabe country star, but it reminded me of two parts of my life. The first was being a teacher at CWL. I often thought it wasn't a real job because I loved it so much. It didn't pay very well, and the hours were long, but the interaction with students and families was wonderful. I met so many great people over the years there. Carol knew I would drive two hours to watch "my kids" play basketball on a Tuesday night. If I didn't have someone to ride with me, she would go along, just so I would have company. I loved it.

The second part of my life is riding my motorcycle. Carol didn't always want to or couldn't ride with me for various reasons. But it is what I love to do, and she understood. She was always supportive of me taking a long bike trip. Part of a successful marriage is to trust your partner and to encourage him/her to do the things we love to do. Carol loved Longaberger. I love to ride. It worked for us. This song just fit today. I hope you enjoy it too.

Day 365
Journal entry by Bill Funnemark — 10/20/2017

A year and a few hours ago, my life changed forever. Watching helplessly as your wife slips into a coma, never to return, will do that to you. I didn't know it at the time, but I lost my love that afternoon along the boardwalk in Myrtle Beach, SC.

This has been a year of many ups and downs. With Carol's brain bleed and subsequent death, I became a widower. This was something I never envisioned. Yes, we all know we are going to die someday, but we don't expect it to happen to someone who is healthy and full of life. Accidents happen and anyone of us could be struck down at any time. But these things happen to other people, not my family.

I have cried and laughed, been lonely and sad, experienced great joy and great sorrow these past 12 months. I made new friends and strengthened old friendships. I've been confused, and levelheaded. I've drawn closer to God and been very angry with God. I've made good decisions and bad ones. But I did survive. I miss my Carol so much, in so many ways but I keep getting up each day and try to do something good. Somedays I'm more successful at it than other days, but I keep trying.

Tomorrow I am riding my Triumph back to Myrtle Beach, SC to where it all began. Some may think it strange or a little creepy, but not me. The resort is a special place for me. These next few days will give me my Bill time, free to do absolutely nothing if I so choose. It will be a time to reflect on the great marriage we had, the many blessings we shared, and to contemplate my new life without Carol.

Life is good for the most part. I miss my sweetheart, I miss being able share special life moments with her, I miss our closeness. I want to tell her that Connor is playing hockey again or that Will caught a touchdown pass tonight or that Trice went out for football this year. I want her to be able to go with me in March for Chad's retirement from the Air Force. I want her to lie on the beach with me and make me take selfies of my food. I want her to pray for me tomorrow as I leave on a motorcycle trip like she always did. Some of my friends have taken on this job from time to time, but it's not the same.

Other than the obvious though, I can't complain. God has been good to me. I just miss my Carol Jean. Good night and thanks for a year of support in so many ways.

An addendum to my last evening's post.

There are many people who have been with me on this journey. First of course is my God. I sometimes feel like He left me hanging, but I know He never left me. My family has been so supportive of my needs and wants, even as they go through their own grief and sense of loss. I have an incredible set of friends, some brand new and others from years ago.

I hesitate to name you for fear of omission, but there are just a few who hold a special place. Ed and Becky have been friends forever and were with Carol and me a year ago and have continued to be with me through this journey. Andy is a high school friend who reached out through many emails of support. Don is a high school classmate, who forced me to keep writing this journal. Suzanne and her family have accepted me as sort of a father, grandfather type figure, and is a fellow widow and she has shared many hours of support and advice. Karen, another widow whom I have known for many years, is a part of my recovery story too. Life would be better if Carol was still here, but she's not. Thanks to all these friends and family who help make my life worth living.

Bill

Day 374
Journal entry by Bill Funnemark — 10/29/2017

It has been over a year now that Carol has been gone. I know she didn't actually die until December 1, 2016, but by this time a year ago, there were very few signs of a recovery, but we hadn't given up hope. Chad had already gone back to Oregon, Mickolyn would be leaving in a couple days and Steph the day after that. We were all still just numb. As hard as it was to see Carol lying there in a coma, it was even harder to say good-bye to my children. They each had to return to their homes and families knowing that they may never see their mom again. Later when more family came and went, I had the same feelings that they were saying good-bye for the last time.

I spent the past few days in Myrtle Beach at Ocean 22 resort, where I stayed a year ago. Many of the staff greeted me and welcomed me home. Ocean 22 became my home for six weeks last year and the staff became almost like family. It was good to be back, memories and all, but it just seemed like something I needed to do. I went to Moe Moon's, the restaurant where Carol and I ate our last lunch. I hit a couple other spots too where we had been together. I didn't go back to the hospital though. That just seemed like a little too much. I did meet with two of Carol's nurses. We had a chance to relive part of those days a year ago, but also what has gone on with me since.

I think a chapter in my life is really over now. I have moved on already in some ways, but this just seems to finalize it. I sold a large portion of Carol's Longaberger collection. I've donated her vast collection of paperback books and started going through her clothes. I still say, "We do this or that" or "We like this or that," but it is becoming more comfortable saying I or me. I still wear my wedding ring, but I don't feel married anymore. I like to look at pictures of the two of us and a lot of the time I can smile while doing so. But there are still plenty of times that looking at memories brings a tear. As I talk to other widow/widowers, I hear the same things from them.

I never intended this journal to go on forever. I thought I was just updating friends and family on my journey. I thought that after Carol died, I would be done writing. Then it was suggested that I keep writing and I did. But now, I think it is time to write my final chapter. I and my family are unique, just as everyone else's family is. Everyone has, or will face, a death of someone very special to them. The circumstances will be unique to you. I'm not the first husband to lose his wife. My dad lost my mom way too early and he continued on, as will I. My children lost their mother, as did I, and they will continue on. There will always be that feeling of loss, that empty place at the table, the missing person at Christmas and on and on. I don't remember a time in my life when Carol was not there, other than this past year. We went to grade school, middle school, high school and Sunday school together. We became a couple in December of 1966 and it ended December of 2016.

I was a little hesitant at first to share my feelings, but now I'm glad I did. It was a way for me to update you on what was happening with Carol and what was going on with me. I hope that everyone who read my journal appreciated my words and I hope that I may have actually helped a few along the way. But now it is time for me to close. As my mom wrote in a letter to be read at her own funeral, I will just say "Auf Wiedersehen" (auf vee der sayen), German for "Until we meet again."

In Conclusion

I had hoped to have my journal ready for publication by now, but these things take longer than I expected. It gives me a chance to update my story. I tried to write my journal as openly and honest as possible. During the trying days at Grand Strand Medical Center and the final days at Algona Good Samaritan Care Center, I did keep some of the truth from most of you. I had a group email to family and a few close friends in which I gave a more pessimistic evaluation of Carol's prognosis. This was a more realistic evaluation of what was going on, but I didn't want to share some of that. I did however share some of these notes earlier in this book. I will just say that I knew very early on that Carol was not going to survive. It just seemed to me that the medical staff was telling me this, even though they never actually did. I just sort of read between the lines.

After Carol had been moved from the NSICU to the stepdown unit, there was no progress. She was just stable. Her case worker talked about a transfer to a rehab center, either in South Carolina or possibly in Iowa. I questioned this as a futile and expensive step. The case worker was very determined to transfer Carol, so I had to take a stand. I asked her lead doctor about Carol's prognosis. I thought she could survive for months or even years in her current state. I asked for his honest appraisal and he told me that Carol would not get better and would not live more than a few weeks. She would get an infection, most likely pneumonia, or else her body would just start shutting down. This was very hard to hear, but in my heart, I already knew this. I still needed to make choices about Carol's care. My family and I agreed on a DNR order and withholding antibiotics. What we could not agree on was keeping her feeding tube in place.

On November 21, 2016, Carol was loaded into an ambulance for her trip home to Algona. The medical staff who rode along were informed on the DNR order. We discussed what would happen if Carol died along the way. They would proceed to the nearest hospital and drop her body there. I would then have to make arrangements for transfer. Before they left Grand Strand, they did disconnect her feeding tube and I assumed this was permanent. The decision had already been made that she would be going into Hospice care once she arrived at Good Samaritan in Algona. One of the hardest choices I had to make came the morning of the 22nd. Mickolyn was at Good Sam to handle paperwork as Carol was admitted, and I was driving myself from Myrtle Beach to home. I got a call from Mickolyn asking about reconnecting the feeding tube. It was clear from Mickolyn's comments that she assumed the feeding tube would be reconnected. I didn't have the energy to argue and I didn't want to go against my children's wishes, but I knew it would just prolong the inevitable. As fate would have it, the feeding tube was doing very little good anyway. Carol's body was not accepting it. Eventually her Hospice nurse removed it because she said it was causing Carol distress. A major decision I had to make was taken out of my hands and family harmony was maintained. Funny how God works.

A lot has happened to me in the nearly two years since that fateful day in Myrtle Beach, October 20, 2016. I've made some wise choices and some foolish ones. I became involved in a relationship with another woman way too soon after Carol's death. This lady is a wonderful woman and one I've known for a long time. She was in a different stage of grief than I was and much more prepared to be dating. I am an adult and should have known how to handle things, but I didn't. So, after an on again off again relationship, we parted company. I didn't handle it very well to say the least.

When we were together and on good terms, we had a lot of fun and she was great to be with. Experts and non-experts alike, warn widows and widowers to not make any sudden, major changes in their lives after the loss of a spouse. I thought I knew what I was doing and failed to heed these warnings. My children warned me to be cautious about getting seriously involved with another woman. Some of my friends said the same thing, as did my pastor. But I thought I knew better. I was lonely and empty and thought I had it all under control. I was wrong. I was not ready for a serious relationship. I disappointed my family and put myself through unnecessary stress. I also lost a friend. I unintentionally hurt her and her family and for this I am very sorry. Maybe in time she will forgive me for the hurt I caused her and we can be friends again.

I confided in my pastor shortly after Carol died that I wasn't sure I ever wanted to remarry. For now, I was looking forward to being single. Don't get me wrong, I would much rather still be married to Carol, but that is not an option. Carol and I were a couple for nearly 50 years. I had dated a few girls in high school before her, but that was a long time ago. I wanted to experience what it is like to be single. I want to have friends, both male and female, and I want to be able to go out with a woman without feeling guilty. There was, and I guess still is, a feeling that I might be showing disrespect for Carol by seeing other women. I don't feel that way very much anymore, but I'm not ready to settle down into a committed, monogamous relationship. I have some really good friends who help fill the void. Some are couples, while others are singles. All are important. My widow friends have a much better understanding of my pain and my needs, but you don't have to be a widow to be a great comfort. Friends are friends, and all are important.

I tried taking off my wedding ring a few times, but it just didn't feel right. After the turmoil of a relationship with KP that didn't work out, I stepped back to look at my life. On May 3rd, 2018 I moved my ring to my right hand. It physically felt weird, but emotionally it just felt right. Symbolically I guess this is a major step, but I didn't think anyone would notice. I went to Mickolyn's house the next day and she noticed right away. A couple other people commented the first time they saw me too. I think I may have given some friends like Suzanne the wrong idea as to my status, but all I meant by removing my ring was that I am no longer married. Time has passed, and it is several months later. I still notice my left ring finger is bare, but it doesn't feel weird anymore.

I have spent a lot of time visiting my family and putting miles on my Triumph. Part of why I travel is to see my family. I want to be able to watch my grandkids play their sports or see their concerts or other activities. These provide a reason to travel. I also take trips just because I like to ride. Once I get to a destination, I may not do much, but I enjoy the ride there and back home. This is an activity Carol knew I enjoyed. She would want me to continue my passion.

How am I doing two years later? For the most part, I am doing well. But almost everyday something will bring a tear to my eye. It could be a song, a billboard, a television program or seeing a loving couple sharing their lives. I can be riding along some rural highway and something will trigger a memory and I will need to stop to dry my eyes. But mostly I am good. Every so often I will have a Carol dream. These have all been happy occasions. Whenever I see her, she looks great and seems so happy. She doesn't seem to understand what has happened. She just smiles and laughs and is glad to see me. I have no idea what these mean and I don't plan to have them analyzed. I'm just going to enjoy them.

This past July my two girls and their families were able to join me in Myrtle beach for a week. The grandkids had never been there and neither had some of the adults. I wish Chad and his family could have joined us, but that just wasn't going to be possible. We had a good time, but there were some hard memories. We all went to lunch one day at Moe Moon's, where Carol had her last lunch. I told the kids the whole story, showed them where we were seated and shared a memory. It was good for me to be there and to be able to share those memories. I'm not sure about my girls. I think it added some closure for all of us though.

01/03/2019

It's just a few days after the two-year anniversary of Carol's death. I have made some very special connections with friends, disappointed a few others, made visits to family across the country, started working as a substitute teacher in the Baxter area, and a few other things. My future plans are starting to take shape but I'm not ready to make them public just yet. I'm getting used to my new normal.

My final words are these. Love your spouse with all your heart and soul. Spend time with him or her, but also spend time apart. Let yourselves be individuals, but always remember you are a couple. For younger people reading this, don't forget why you fell in love. Keep dating each other. Get a babysitter and the two of you go out. All too soon it will be just the two of you again. Carol and I dated for fifty years and loved each other more in October 2016 than we did back in 1970 when we got married. Don't wait until later to do the things you want to do. Even though we only had a short time together after we had both retired, we did a lot of things for many years before. God has been good to me. I don't know what He has in store for me in the next few months, few years or the rest of my life. I'm trying to keep my eyes open to what God would have me do. One of these days will be my time to rejoin Carol in Heaven. Until that time, I hope to live my remaining days on Earth to fullest.

Thank you, Carol, for a wonderful life together. I will love you forever.

Bill

Epilogue

May 27, 2019

I have a feeling I will never finish this book. My life continues take many twists and turns. A few months ago I was ready to sell my house and move closer to Mickolyn. I had a potential buyer that seemed like the perfect solution. I was convinced I should make the move. But that deal fell through, at least for now. For now, I still live in Algona. Maybe I'm not ready to move. I have not closed any doors, but things are just on hold for now. I'm feeling more comfortable with my house and maybe I will just stay there for now.

I had mentioned somewhere in my journal that I planned to run my 24th marathon, but that never happened. I could never find the right one or the time to train. I have had a desire for a long time to be able to run a marathon after I turned 70. I found the perfect marathon for this goal. I have entered the Air Force Marathon in Dayton, Ohio. The race is on September 21, 2019, nine days after my 70th birthday and on what would have been Carol's 71st birthday. She won't be there physically, but she will with me in spirit. She will be cheering me every step of the way. I'm running this one, number 24, for you Babe. I still love you and miss you so much.

This time I really am done writing!!

Bill

CPSIA information can be obtained
at www.ICGtesting.com
Printed in the USA
FFHW011926220719
53798684-59499FF